The Gila Wilderness Area

THE GILA WILDERNESS AREA

A HIKING GUIDE

JOHN A. MURRAY

UNIVERSITY OF NEW MEXICO PRESS
Albuquerque

To my brothers, Mike and Bill

Design: Milenda Nan Ok Lee

Library of Congress Cataloging in Publication Data

Murray, John A., 1954–
  The Gila Wilderness Area.

  Bibliography: p.
  Includes index.
  1. Hiking—New Mexico—Gila Lower Box Wilderness—
Guide-books. 2. Natural history—New Mexico—Gila
Lower Box Wilderness. 3. Gila Lower Box Wilderness
(N.M.)—Guide-books. I. Title.
GV199.42.N62G556 1988   917.89′692   87-35753
ISBN 0-8263-1067-2 (pbk.)

In that country which lies around the headwaters of the Gila River I was reared. This range was our fatherland; among these mountains our wigwams were hidden; the scattered valleys contained our fields; the boundless prairies, stretching away on every side, were our pastures; the rocky caverns were our burying places. I was the fourth in a family of eight children—four boys and four girls. . . . As a babe I rolled on the dirt floor of my father's teepee, hung in my tsoch at my mother's back, or suspended from the bough of a tree. I was warmed by the sun, rocked by the winds, and sheltered by the trees as other Indian babes. When a child my mother taught me the legends of our people; taught me of the sun and sky, the moon and stars, the clouds and storms. She also taught me to kneel and pray to Usen for strength, health, wisdom, and protection. We never prayed against any person, but if we had aught against any individual we ourselves took vengeance. We were taught that Usen does not care for the petty quarrels of men. My father had often told me of the brave deeds of our warriors, of the pleasures of the chase, and the glories of the warpath. With my brothers and sisters I played about my father's home. Sometimes we played at hide-and-seek among the rocks and pines . . . while our parents worked in the field. . . . Sometimes we would hide away from our mother to see if she could find us, and often when thus concealed go to sleep and perhaps remain hidden for many hours. When we were old enough to be of real service we went to the fields with our parents; not to play, but to toil. When the crops were to be planted we broke the ground with wooden hoes. We planted the corn in straight rows, the beans among the corn, and the melons and pumpkins in irregular order over the field. We cultivated these crops as there was need.

—Geronimo, *Autobiography* (1905)

Contents

Preface

Now, when I was a little chap, I had a passion for maps. I would look for hours . . . and lose myself in all the glories of exploration. At that time there were many blank spaces on the earth, and when I saw one that looked particularly inviting on a map . . . I would put my finger on it and say, "When I grow up I will go there."

—Joseph Conrad, *Heart of Darkness*

The idealism expressed in the wilderness concept, of areas purposefully left untrammeled by man, has made all Americans visiting these regions feel just a little more proud of their birthright. It embodies the finest of our national qualities: our reverence for life, our high-spirited love of adventure, our generosity, our curiosity, and our basic optimism. The frontier comes alive again in these remote primeval places, and we share once more as common players in that noble history: of hardy Pilgrims making first landfall on a perilous coast, of Daniel Boone striking out boldly into the great unknown beyond the Cumberland Gap, of Lewis and Clark exploring regions where no white man had ever gone, of determined homesteaders braving the Oregon Trail in their sturdy Conestoga wagons, and of Neal Armstrong landing his spacecraft on the bright barren shores of a strange new world in the heavens. We are a people whose character was quarried from the rock of travail, forged in the crucible of change, and refined among the elements of risk and chance. The wilderness experience, both in its egalitarian spirit and democratic opportunity, is so much a part of our history as to almost be synonymous with it. We are, quite literally, a frontier society, and our history is largely a history of the frontier.

Perhaps no other wilderness area in the Southwest or elsewhere so much embodies and reflects this national history and natural philosophy as does the Gila. Many of the important events in the development of the region, from the first expedition of Coronado in 1541 to the more recent raids of Geronimo, occurred either directly in the Gila Wilderness Area or in the immediate vicinity. The cliff dwellings of the ancient Mogollon civilization are present here, as are the campsites and battlegrounds of the Apache and the U.S. Cavalry, the abandoned cabins of pioneers, the secret retreats of outlaws, and the remnants of once active mines. A peculiar human richness abounds throughout the Gila country, and the hills and valleys resonate with a multitude of historical associations while at the same time offering the spectacular beauty of the desert uplands.

The Gila Wilderness encompasses and protects the headwaters of the three forks of the Gila River which with their major tributaries deeply dissect a large mesalike region formed primarily through volcanic deposition. Toward the west are the extremely rugged Mogollon Mountains. To the north are several isolated peaks and broad divides. Eastward is the appropriately named Black Range and to the south is the Pinos Altos Range, and, beyond that, the dry flats leading down into Mexico. Elevations range from 4,800 feet near the confluence of Turkey Creek and the Gila River to 10,895 feet on Whitewater Baldy. In a single day a hiker can climb from an Upper Sonoran canyon dominated by cholla, agave, prickly pear cactus, Arizona sycamore, and grey oak, to a Subalpine coniferous forest indistinguishable from those found in the far north of Canada. The ascent of more than a mile upward leads past lava pinnacles and steep cliffs, through piñon and juniper woodlands, ponderosa forests, grassy meadows, high prairies, and aspen parklands.

Because of its proximity to Mexico, which is only some 80 miles to the south, backcountry travelers will note several plant and animal species more common to Mexico and Central America than North America existing side-by-side with those commonly found throughout the Rocky Mountains. Exotic animal visitors from this lower region include the jaguar, which resembles the Old World leopard; the coatimundi, or ring-tailed cat; and the javelina, which is a type of wild swine. Wildlife indigenous to the Rockies includes the pronghorn antelope, the mule deer, the white-tailed deer, the elk or wapiti, the black bear, and the mountain lion, as well as such avifauna as the quail, dove, owl, and turkey. Plants on their northern range here include the Schott's yucca, Chihuahua pine, Apache pine, Arizona cypress, Arizona walnut, Arizona madrone, Arizona sycamore, point-leaf manzanita, alligator juniper, and Emory oak. Several unusual species of animal and plant are found here as well, including the subspecies of the whip-tailed lizard, in which the female clones herself from an unfertilized gamete; several locally rare birds, including the osprey and the scissor-tailed flycatcher; and 11 species of orchid. Few places in North America contain such a rich and diverse biotic community which reflects the influences of two separate continents and the blending of two rather distinctive sets of flora and fauna.

As a federal entity, the Gila Wilderness is unique in several respects. The area was originally set aside in 1899 as the Gila River Forest Reserve, some 13 years before New Mexican statehood. In 1905 responsibility for forest reserves was shifted from the USDI to the USDA. The next administrative change came in 1907 when the designation of "forest reserve," which reserved the land from public domain in order to regulate its use for the good of the majority instead of a few, was changed to "national forest." The Gila subsequently became the nation's (and the world's) first wilderness area, established in 1924 largely through the efforts of Aldo Leopold. There were 755,000 acres in the initial allotment approved by the Forest Service. The national forest in which the Wilderness is located is now one of the largest in America at 3,320,135 acres. The Gila Wilderness Area (now 569,792 acres) is when coupled with the adjacent Aldo Leopold Wilderness Area (211,300 acres) one of the largest wild areas in the desert Southwest, protecting over 1,000 square miles of desert uplands. It encompasses all the diverse headwaters of the Gila River, as well as associated tributaries and mountainous terrain. Besides protecting the habitat of several endangered species, the Gila also enjoys the distinction of containing the largest continuous stand of virgin ponderosa pine in wilderness in the world.

The problem, or challenge, facing the Gila and areas like it in the future is primarily one of use. The regional population has soared in recent years with the large scale exodus from the East and Midwest to the sunbelt states and is projected by authorities to grow substantially for some time to come. If it is true that the need for wilderness is proportional to population and urbanization, then the Gila will undoubtedly face greater demands as time passes. In other wilderness areas, such as the Indian Peaks Wilderness Area located near Denver, Colorado, increased use has resulted in unacceptable levels of environmental damage which has led to further backcountry restrictions which, in turn, has limited access. As access is denied, the quality of life inevitably declines, with the ever-present possibility that related social problems in the cities and the suburbs, particularly those among the young, will increase. The answer is clear. These areas must be preserved intact and in pristine condition and, if anything, increased in size, diversity, and number, providing a much-needed buffer in the crowded centuries to follow between man and his fellow men.

This book was written for both the serious hiker and the campground visitor to broaden their perspective on the natural history of the area, to answer a few of their many questions about the interesting human history, and to provide a source upon which to make decisions about which trails to hike. Because of the vast size of the Gila and the comparative importance of various trails, this book is selective, presenting only the major trails (some 24 in number) which offer well over 300 miles of backcountry hiking. These will undoubtedly be sufficient for the majority of visitors, since the remaining trails sometimes have less scenic significance, a few are in a state of disuse or decline, and some are no longer maintained by the Forest Service. Others of these remaining trails, however, are quite nice and offer opportunities for solitude.

Twentieth-century science has shown that humankind's existence and role in the cosmos is not omnipotent, immutable, or, in all likelihood, even particularly unique. We are, rather, responsible participants in a fragile and tentative experiment of nature. Science and technology have not, as some originally feared, made wilderness obsolete but have on the contrary given new significance to our relationship with nature and have informed that partnership with an understanding unprecedented in the history of the human race. We now see that the effort to protect the wilds is not simply an enterprise designed to establish playgrounds for the young and hardy, but is instead vitally linked with the vast conundrum of life in this world. "As soon as we take one thing by itself," wrote John Muir, "we find it hitched to everything in the universe." *Homo sapiens* is, despite all the tinsel and trappings of civilization, still just a carbon-based organism spun in the same web of life as the spider and the swallowtail, brother to the bear, cousin of the raccoon, and distant relative of the tiny water shrew. The wilderness in this sense holds the key to understanding our past, as well as ensuring that we as a species continue to have a future.

ACKNOWLEDGMENTS

I would like to thank those members of the Gila National Forest who assisted me in the preparation of this book, including Kenneth C. Scoggin, Forest Supervisor; Michael G. Gardner, District Ranger; Ronald Bradsby, District Ranger; Bill Luera, District F.M.O.; Dave Peters, Wilderness Supervisor; and various personnel at the Wilderness Ranger Station, at the National Monument, and on the trail who were always most courteous and helpful. Thanks also to Doc Campbell of Gila Hot Springs and his wife, Ida, for their hospitality in the summer of 1983.

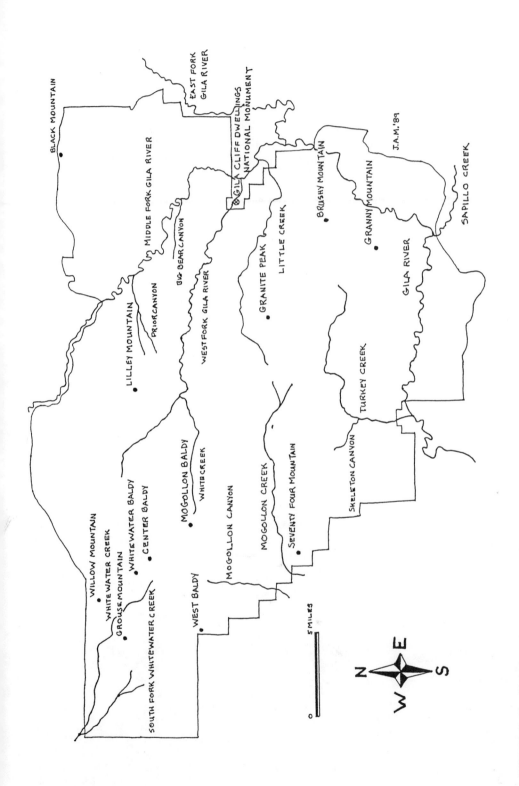

Part I.

The Natural History

Back of the camp we saw 30 antelope feeding on the mesa to the south. The whole immensity of the Gila basin lay spread before us in a sunset so quiet you could hear a cricket chirp. It was a sight worth the whole trip.

> —Aldo Leopold, Late Fall, 1929 (private journals as cited by Elizabeth McFarland in *Wilderness of the Gila*)

Ecology

The ecology of the Gila Wilderness is complex and diverse, reflecting not only the larger continental influences of the Rocky Mountains, the Chihuahuan Desert, and the Sierra Madre Mountains, but also the local effects of altitude, exposure, soil, macro and microclimate, landforms, and various physical events. The entire region—its mountains, mesas, and river canyons—is geographically situated in such a way that it has become a transition zone between the cool/wet Rockies and the warm/dry Chihuahuan Desert and Sierra Madre Mountains. It is from an ecological standpoint triply endowed and enriched by these three influences, which overlap and blend over the terrain like the shaded circles of a Venn diagram, forming stands, continuums, associations, communities, and ecotones.

The Gila Wilderness, like an enormous quilt patched together very slowly over the ages, is fairly well broken up into an intermixed array of eight major vegetative types based on dominant species: coniferous forest (primarily spruce-fir), aspen forest, ponderosa pine forest, oak woodland, piñon-juniper woodland, grassland, deciduous woodland (riparian), and brush. As the Great Basin has its sagebrush, the Rockies its blue spruce, the Mohave Desert its Joshua tree, the Sonoran Desert its saguaro cactus, and the Chihuahuan Desert its lechugilla agave, each species standing as a popular symbol for the region as a whole, the Gila Wilderness is probably best known and remembered for the vast forests of ponderosa pine which form its most prominent vegetative type. The upper elevations (from 9,000 feet to 10,895 feet), for the most part in the Mogollon Mountains, are dominated by dense, closed canopy forests, primarily of Douglas fir and Engelmann's spruce, with aspen groves, wet meadows, and grass parks scattered through them. Midrange altitudes (7,000 feet to 9,000 feet), associated with the mesa tops and their network of streams and canyons, support a more complex and heterogenous pattern of vegetation: ponderosa pine forests, small aspen groves, oak woodland, grassland, piñon-juniper woodland, some deciduous woodlands (riparian), and some brush. Lower altitudes (well below 7,000 feet), confined to the river canyons, support a riparian community of moisture-loving deciduous trees, evergreen oaks, bushes, grasses, cacti, flowers, and herbs. Exposure is one of the more important factors to vegetation in the Gila Wilderness with as a general rule piñon-juniper favoring south-facing slopes and ponderosa pine found on north-facing slopes. At higher elevations, Douglas fir prefers north-facing slopes, with aspen, a successional type, found on any exposure where the pines have been removed by nature or man.

The single most significant factor in determining the ecology of the Gila Wilderness is precipitation which varies depending on location but rarely exceeds more than 17 water inches of rain per year on average. Running water is conspicuously absent in the higher ridges, peaks, and saddles of the Gila country, and, in some regions, near-desert conditions prevail. Seasonal drought is common at the semi-desert lower elevations, and nearly every spring and fall plants in these areas suffer stress from lack of moisture. Generally summer and winter moisture is very deficient two or three years out of each ten-year period. This has altered the plant life and their strategies for survival. Areas over 7,000 feet normally receive sufficient precipitation, as evidenced by the presence of trees and plants that cannot cope with the harsher conditions of lower elevations. However, even at these midelevations and higher, droughts do occur periodically, which significantly affect plant growth and the animals that are dependent on those plants.

The second most important factor to the ecology of this region is physical location, particularly with respect to altitude. As one climbs upward through the rugged terrain of the Gila, the air temperature drops about one degree Fahrenheit for every 250 to 300 feet ascended. A climb of over 5,000 feet from the Turkey Creek confluence with the Gila River to Mogollon Baldy can be accompanied on an average summer day by a drop in the air temperature from 90 degrees to 70 degrees Fahrenheit and a three-fold increase in mean annual precipitation. Additionally, for every 1,000 feet gained in altitude, the effect on vegetation is roughly comparable to a journey northward of 300 miles. On that same hike, then, an ascent of 5,000 feet travels from a Sonoran life zone more common to that part of Mexico for which it is named to a Subalpine or Canadian life zone, virtually identical to that which is found 1,500 miles farther north in the Canadian Rockies.

Like all ecosystems, the simple function of this diverse and sometimes confusing array of plants and animals, food chains and energy paths, feedback systems and regulatory cycles, is to capture and use the light of the sun. This process is accomplished with the assistance of the nitrogen, oxygen, and carbon dioxide provided by the air, the life-giving water furnished by the atmosphere and by natural springs and streams, and the chemicals and materials found in the earth itself. Each organism in the Gila, from the lowly crustose lichen to the magnificent golden eagle, occupies a particular functional niche in the community analogous to the particular job a single human being might have in human society. Where in human society we have the flow of money which facilitates the transfer of goods and services and thus sustains the population, in these natural communities we have the flow of energy from the sun through the autotrophic communities (plants) where it is initially captured through photosynthesis to the heterotrophic component (the animals, including herbivores, omnivores, and carnivores). All food chains end with the decomposers, organisms that reduce plants and animals into the simplest substances, available again for the food chain.

For the purpose of discussion in this book, the Gila Wilderness has been broadly divided into three areas, which will then be further subdivided: the Mogollon Mountains, the Uplands, and the Canyon Bottoms. While not a common form of classification, this will undoubtedly prove to be conceptually helpful to those seeking an understanding of the region. Each of these zones is separate and unique from a vegetative standpoint and yet is still vitally linked with the other zones. Although the function of the component plants and animals, as well as of the systems themselves, seems relatively easy to quantify and organize, the overall design and purpose of the whole as well as of its constituent individuals remains forever elusive, the proper domain not of physical science and natural history but of philosophy, religion, and poetry. That nature is more mysterious and elusive, more complex and yet more simple, than our notions of it is in the end cause for celebration and not regret.

THE MOGOLLON MOUNTAINS

To some, the most beautiful forests of the Gila are the dense coniferous stands of Douglas fir and Englemann's spruce found in the Mogollon Mountains and elsewhere in the Wilderness where elevation, soil type, and moisture lend themselves to this sort of climax forest. Ecological conditions in this area can be compared with those found in the far north, before the trees thin out and become dwarfed in the boreal regions at the southern fringes of the arctic tundra. Authorities refer to this sort of community as a Subalpine forest, Canadian forest, or spruce-fir climax forest. These dark and spire-crowned forests stretch uniformly across the steep valleys and ridges of the Mogollons for many miles, broken only by successional stands of quaking aspen, occasional grass parks, and rock outcroppings. This is often a truly primeval forest whose character has changed very little for many hundreds, if not thousands, of years. It flourishes throughout the West, from the Yukon to the Sierra Madre, wherever the rough terrain, bouldery substratum, and low commercial timber values have discouraged exploitation and wherever relatively moist environments have kept fires to a minimum.

Many generations of trees have lived, died, and fallen over in these long persisting stands and the wind throw of both living and dead trees is common. The resulting tangle of stumps and fallen logs in all stages of decay makes this area a favored range for the reclusive elk. Some individual specimens of fir and spruce are over 3 feet in diameter and well over 100 feet tall. Many times they are covered with "Old Man's Beard" (*Usnea*), a gray-green form of lichen (actually an aerial, symbiotic union of a fungi and an algae) similar in appearance to the Spanish moss that festoons the live oaks of the deep South, which gives the forest an eerie quality like the mythical midsummer woods of Shakespeare's Oberon and Titania. In the *Usnea*, as in other lichens, the fungus forms the structure or body of the organism, providing shelter for the colonies of microscopic algal cells. The algae contain chlorophyll and through photosynthesis provide carbohydrates for both partners. The fungus also absorbs minerals from the surfaces to which the lichen is attached and moisture which the algae require for photosynthesis from the air. The lichens attach themselves to the trees

Down timber in the Mogollon Mountains along the Crest Trail. This is classic spruce-fir subalpine habitat. Photograph by John Murray

by threadlike fungal rhizoids. Lichens are some of the oldest and simplest plants in the world and perhaps because of that they have and will continue to endure.

The snow remains long in these deeply shaded Subalpine forests and adds to the moisture during the dry months of May and June, keeping the community relatively wet and cool until the summer rains begin in July. In spite of the perpetual twilight, herbs and shrubs as well as many flowers, seedlings, and saplings grow on the forest floor. The Apache often ate the various berries found in this forest as well as the inner bark of the pine trees when other foods were not available. Some of the aspen trees in the Mogollon Mountains, such as those on the Crest Trail above Sandy Point, are extremely large, sometimes attaining diameters of two feet. The aspen tree, though, is only an ephemeral visitor to these climax forests and normally dies in its eighth or ninth decade.

Apparently the aspen was more prevalent in the Mogollons in the past when forest fires were not controlled as were larger tracts of grassland elsewhere in the Wilderness. Both have dwindled as fire suppression policies have eliminated the natural homeostatic mechanism of forest fire. The aspen, like the lodgepole pine, is a successional tree. It will not form a true climax forest. Even those stands that seem quite beautiful and permanent, like the extremely large forest on the northwest flank of Whitewater Baldy facing Hummingbird Saddle, will one day be replaced by the fir and the spruce. The aspen is a "nurse" tree for the coniferous species and quickly repopulates those areas recently exposed by fire or logging. In its shade the young pine seedlings and saplings find protection and can grow. A transitional tree, the aspen becomes susceptible to disease and insect infestation as it approaches the century mark. At that point aspens are normally replaced by the coniferous trees that have grown up beside them. The aspen has the lovely Latin appellation *Populus tremuloides*, which alludes to the soft tremor of the leaves as they shimmer and shake on the slightest breeze. At times this sound is so pronounced that a hiker hearing the wind in the aspen over a ridge might mistakenly think there is a rushing stream on the other side.

The aspen grove generally has more herbs, flowers, shrubs, and ferns than the Subalpine evergreen forest, because the canopy is more open and more light reaches the forest floor. Aspen can also tolerate surprisingly dry and exposed locations, adapting by becoming dwarfed and scrubby. Many times the aspen trees are curiously deformed, as for example those found on the Crest Trail just before Hummingbird Saddle. Their trunks assume shapes resembling doglegs, S-curves, elbows, and knees. The deformity occurs in the lower part of the trunk, no more than four or five feet from the ground. Above this level the smooth white trunks assume the normal immaculate attitude of the aspen. This phenomena results from the compressive and creeping effects of the massive snow drifts that linger through May and June, overlapping with the beginning of seasonal growth. Sometimes one can also detect where hungry elk have nibbled at the bark in lean years, where both elk and deer have rubbed the velvet from their antlers, and where bears have territorially marked the trunks with their claws.

Eagles and hawks nest in the pockets and crannies of cliffs found in

An aspen grove near Hummingbird Spring in the Mogollon Mountains.
(Photograph by John Murray)

this zone, as well as in extremely tall trees. The Apache would some-times trap these birds by luring them to the ground with tethered rabbits. The feathers which were then collected were used in cere-monial headdresses and for other religious and social purposes. The Apache also sought out the burned bark of trees in these areas that had been struck by lightning. They would wrap the splinters in yards and yards of cloth and carry them, as talismans possessing special powers that would bring good fortune and strength to those who owned them.

As a general rule, there are fewer wild animals in dense forests such as are found in the Mogollon Mountains than in areas with more open parks, grass meadows, and high pastures. Fire suppression policies have resulted in a very closed ecological situation with little of the transition/edge areas that are vital to wildlife. This is probably most notable in the ungulate populations. A closed canopy forest, for example, may only support 3 or 4 deer per square mile, whereas an area of mixed forest and meadow may support as many as 15 or 20 deer per square mile. Still, the area supports healthy herds of mule deer and a growing number of elk, which were initially transplanted into the area in 1925 after the original Merriam's elk were hunted into extinction.

The Uplands

The primary vegetative type of the region called here the Uplands (all of that country between canyon bottoms and the higher mountains) is the ponderosa pine forest. The finest view of this extensive region (which also includes components of piñon-juniper, oak woodland, grassland, and brush) is afforded from the Copperas Vista turnoff on New Mexico 15, approximately five miles north of the turnoff to Lake Roberts and San Lorenzo. This expansive panorama includes the headwaters of the Middle Fork and the West Fork in the far background and the Gila River in the foreground. From Granny Mountain on the far left to Lilley Mountain at a greater distance to Black Mountain almost due north, the heart of the Gila Wilderness, of the region called here the Uplands, is visible in one glance. To the uninformed observer, this region appears vast, austere, and inhospitable. Even the briefest of surveys carried out away from the roads, however, reveals a rich and complex diversity of ecosystems, all of which are remarkably adapted to the harsh exigencies and challenges of the high desert environment.

Geographic features are varied and formidable, ranging from peaks and ridges to gorges and canyons to gently rolling interstream uplands. In places, these natural barriers and physical intrusions result in significant floral discontinuity. In other areas, they are supportive of the homogenous pattern of vegetation—the ponderosa pine forest—commonly associated with the highlands of the desert Southwest. As a general rule, the piñon-juniper association is found on south-facing slopes. In places where the climate is too arid to support trees or the soil and steepness is not conducive to their growth, a grass-brush community is found. The ponderosa pine is normally found on north-facing slopes. Grasslands occur frequently on rolling, relatively flat ridge tops and gentle, south-facing slopes. Oak woodlands with a grassy understory are also found at lower elevations, predominately on south-facing slopes.

The individual stands of ponderosa pine differ significantly from one another, with respect to the associated species that are present, the degree of dominance of the pine, and the history of the stand. Young ponderosa stands, those that are overgrowing an area once lumbered

Stands of Ponderosa pine dominate in many areas of the uplands. Photograph taken on the West Fork Trail after first the river crossing. (Photograph by John Murray)

or cleared by fire, are typically quite dense, but the trees rapidly perish in the intense competition for light and space. Consequently, older stands become more open and parklike. On dry slopes the stands are open with a few shrubs, a sparse ground cover of bunch grass, and a few herbs and flowers. In the typical mature stand, tree crowns do not generally meet and tree heights range from 50 to 100 feet. The trees are often clumped and scattered in small groups separated by parklike openings. The deep accumulation of needles which forms under the pines sometimes makes it difficult for herbs and grasses to grow. Generally speaking, the ponderosa prefers a well-developed soil, a gently rolling or even flat surface, and a higher elevation and greater moisture than found on south-facing slopes where the piñon-juniper system flourishes.

Ponderosa pine often lives among the Douglas firs, especially on the upper reaches and north-facing slopes of its habitat. Similarly, it can be found among the juniper and oak occasionally when it ventures down in altitude and onto south-facing slopes. Where conditions are particularly favorable, as is often the case in the Gila Wilderness, the ponderosa pine forms a climax stand, that is, a stand in a state of equilibrium that will persist intact from century to century. This most often occurs on a rolling surface with a well-developed soil, in which the understory is almost nonexistent, offering only a sparse cover of herbs and much bare ground exposed to the atmosphere. To many, it is these pure stands of ponderosa pines, the scent of their needles, the sound of the wind in their boughs, that most captures the essence of the Gila Wilderness.

The second most important vegetative type in this region is the piñon-juniper woodland, which predominates on south-facing slopes which have too little soil and water for ponderosa pine or Douglas fir, but too much of both for semidesert vegetation. The piñon nut is an important food source to animals in this ecosystem, from wood rats to black bears, and historically was collected by the Mogollon and the Apache. The piñon nut is still very much enjoyed by people living in the region. The alligator juniper, so named because of the reptilian texture of its bark, produces fat berries in the fall which were once ground into mush and cakes by the Indians. A fragrant wax was boiled out of the berries' coating. The Emory oak, found in portions of the piñon-juniper woodland, grows extensively in Mexico, Arizona, and New Mexico. The acorn crop of the oak is probably as important to wildlife as the piñon nuts. The acorns of the Emory oak are sweet and tasty, almost free of tannin, and often sold in food markets in Mexico. Three other important plants in this ecosystem include the Schott's yucca, or Spanish dagger, whose buds, flowers, and young flower stalks were eaten raw or boiled by the Apache; the palmer agave, whose heads were steamed and eaten; and the mesquite, whose beans were consumed. Pointleaf manzanita, a member of the heath family also found in these areas, produces a miniature apple (hence the Spanish name *manzanita*) which was used to make a good jelly. Finally, the prickly pear cactus, common in these woodlands, produces a fruit that was treasured by the Apache and provides an important food in the autumn for the black bear. As can be seen, the piñon-juniper woodland, probably more so than the coniferous forest, the aspen forest, or the ponderosa pine forest, contributed more to the survival of early man in this region than any other ecosystem. It was the Apache version of a modern supermarket with everything from nuts and berries to fruits and fresh meat in the form of rabbit, turkey, and mule deer.

Grasslands are common in this region, in association with Gambel's oak and Emory oak woodlands, piñon-juniper woodlands, ponderosa pine forests, and by themselves as extensive prairies. North Mesa offers an excellent example of the latter. Grasslands historically played an important role in the development of the region, providing extensive natural pastures for the grazing of sheep and cattle. Today, they continue to provide grazing opportunities for these two domestic species, as well as for antelope, white-tailed deer, mule deer, and elk. Important animals on the grasslands include the harvester ant, whose distinct mounds dot the landscape, and the prairie dog, whose burrows and villages provide further points of interest. Both animals serve vital functions, aerating the soil with their digging, improving drainage, and increasing the distribution of organic matter by burying surface vegetation. In one study in northern Colorado at a site with 25 prairie dogs per acre, the soil in the mounds when measured weighed over three tons. Both rattlesnakes and bull snakes are found in and near these villages, and eagles and hawks also feed in these areas. The female prairie dogs may give birth to several litters of a dozen or more offspring every year, but many of these are used by predators farther up the food chain as a primary protein source.

The Canyon Bottoms

The central force and feature of the Canyon Bottoms is running water in the form of the streams and rivers whose currents have created these barrancas. Over the geological ages these currents have cut out and enlarged the channels that define the geography of the region and have brought life to it. In places they exposed volcanic and sedimentary rock strata that tell of even earlier periods of history in the region. Because precipitation, the source of all runoff and subsurface water, varies so much seasonally, the rate and volume of streamflow in the Gila Wilderness fluctuates widely, from flood conditions to dry streambed. Water acts not only to carry precipitation and snowmelt to lower ground and to mold the bedrock through which it flows, but also to transport nutrients and waste products downstream, further benefiting the natural community. Most of the major streams and rivers in the Gila are defined as fast or swiftly flowing bodies of water, typical of those found throughout the world in mountainous country with velocities of 50 centimeters per second or greater. At this velocity the current removes all particles less than five millimeters in diameter and leaves behind a stony bottom. In fact most streambeds in the Gila are composed of naked rock, fine sand, or smoothly sculpted cobblestone beds.

Two types of habitat are found in the streams and rivers of the Gila Wilderness: the turbulent riffle, which actually forms rapids in places, and the quiet pool. These two features alternate back and forth as the water flows down the canyon. The riffles are the site of the primary production in the stream. Here, organisms known as *aufwuchs* assume dominance and occupy a position in the food chain similar to phytoplankton in lakes and ponds. They consist of diatoms, blue and green algae, and water moss. This algal growth is ephemeral because of the scouring action of water and debris in the current. The pools just downstream are sites for decomposition and form catch basins for various organic materials, like the dead algae. Pools are the major site for free carbon dioxide production during the summer and fall which is necessary for the maintenance of a constant supply of bicarbonate in solution. Without the pools, the photosynthesis that takes place in the riffles would deplete those bicarbonates and result in smaller and smaller quantities of available carbon dioxide downstream.

A variety of insects lives in the riffles, including the nymphs of mayflies, caddisflies, true flies, stoneflies, and alderflies. The dominant insects inhabiting the pools are burrowing mayfly nymphs, dragonflies, water beetles, damselflies, and water striders. The trout inhabit both areas and feed on all of these insects as well as mice, frogs, snakes, birds, and small muskrats, depending on their size and appetite. A good trout stream is about 50 percent pools and 50 percent riffles. Coexisting with these trout are bass, catfish, minnows, dace, chubs, and suckers. The trout, like much of the aquatic life in these fast-moving streams, has a streamlined body which offers light resistance to the current. Because of its smooth design and muscular bodies, the trout can inhabit even the fastest riffle water.

Most of the smaller insects have flattened bodies and broad flat limbs, with which they can cling to stones and debris at the bottom. Typically the eyes are dorsally located and the gills are platelike. Some forms of life, such as the caddisfly, carry portable houses in this predator-filled realm to protect them from the many dangers. The plants show similar adaptive strategies. The water moss and heavily branched filamentous algae, for example, are held to rocks by strong holdfasts that are supple and durable enough to withstand any current. Additionally, the algae are covered with a slippery gelatinous coating much like the slippery membrane found on fish. Downstream the channels are wider and the waters are not nearly as swift as in the Gila country near the headwaters. The worst threat to these upstream rivers and streams is siltation and flashflooding (which results in some cases from fire suppression on the terrestrial forests) and the lingering effects of past mining, overgrazing, and lumbering. A dam on the Gila would obviously have disastrous consequences for these aquatic communities.

The life around these streams is rich and diverse. The streams and rivers are to the Gila Wilderness what the arteries and veins are to the human body, carrying and distributing life and nutrients to the Wilderness's far distant realms and regions. Both plants and animals migrate up and down the canyons, invading and colonizing new areas and restoring them after they have been destroyed by man or nature. The riparian woodlands contain trees, shrubs, and flowers found nowhere else in the Gila Wilderness, for nowhere else can these

Arizona sycamore beside sheer canyon wall on the West Fork of the Gila River. (Photograph by Charles William Murray, Junior)

moisture-loving species survive. These include such species as the sycamore, walnut, maple, ash, cottonwood, willow, alder, boxelder, wild grape, Virginia creeper, strawberry, raspberry, wild potato, and wild onion. Animal species include frogs, salamanders, muskrat, beaver, javelina, deer, osprey, kingfishers, egrets, herons, ducks, and geese. Many other plant and animal species live in the fringes of these rich woodlands or travel through it often during the course of their lives.

It was the streams and rivers that first attracted men to this area thousands of years ago. They found deep topsoils in which they could plant their crops of bean, squash, pumpkins, and corn; natural caves formed by erosion in which to live; and plentiful game, such as turkey and deer, to hunt. Periodic floods cleared out the thick brush and debris along the rivers and kept them open and parklike. Weather was less severe than in the high mountains or the low desert. It was a good place to live and remains a good place to visit today. Practically all visitors to the Gila Wilderness use the canyons in their backcountry travels.

On north-facing slopes in the lower canyons, ponderosa pine predominates, and, on south-facing slopes the piñon-juniper association is found. Areas of grass and brush are also found on south-facing slopes, including at the lowest elevations areas of semidesert scrub and brush, with such plant species as agave, yucca, various cacti, creosote, Apache plume, and sagebrush. These areas are similar ecologically to those found far to the south in the deserts of the Mohave, Sonora, and Chihuahua. Soils are poor, exposure to the elements severe, and the presence of water scarce. The Gila River may be running at full bank 30 yards down the hill, but in these zones, it might as well be a thousand miles away. These areas remind us of the importance of water in the Gila Wilderness and of the fragility of life in these semidesert areas, where the loss of only several inches of precipitation a year can endanger the whole vast web of life which is dependent upon it.

Flora and Fauna

The Gila Wilderness is the home for many of the plants and animals commonly found in the Rocky Mountains, as well as a few of those more at home in Mexico and Central America than in North America. In this sense, it is a very rich biotic community, mixing as it does the diverse life of two distinctive regions of the hemisphere. Because of pressure from civilization, many species recently present in the area are now extincct, such as the grizzly bear, the timber wolf, the river otter, the Gila turkey, the Merriam's elk, and several fish species. The jaguar and coatimundi are occasional visitors from the south. Javelinas seem to have established permanent populations in a few areas. Reptiles and amphibians are found in abundance. Avifauna is varied and plentiful. Many indigenous species of fish still persist among transplanted species. Travelers should avoid picking wildflowers since many are quite rare and most wilt quickly anyway. Additionally this is also an illegal activity.

MAMMALS.   The most prevalent and important large mammal in the wilderness is the mule deer, which can be found everywhere, from the lowest canyons to the highest mountain peaks. They are easily distinguished by their sleek grey to brown bodies, their big ears (for which they are named), and the large bifurcated antlers on the bucks. Adults normally weigh less than those found in the Rocky Mountains, averaging 200 pounds. The bucks shed their antlers in January and February each year while on their winter range in the lower piñon-juniper communities. A few weeks later they begin to grow their new antlers which are encased in "velvet," a kind of furry live skin which is rubbed off against branches after the antlers have turned to bone. The antlers are used by the bucks in shows of prowess during the rut which occurs in the fall when the does are fertile. Fawns are born in the spring. Deer are browsers, feeding on brush. They are most active in the period around dawn and dusk. During the summer the deer commonly separate by sex, with the mature bucks inhabiting more remote and rugged terrain and the does, fawns, and younger deer banding together in less isolated areas. In addition to the mule deer, white-tailed deer also inhabit the Gila Wilderness, notable as their

Bull snakes keep rodent populations down and also prey on rattlesnakes.
(Photograph by John Murray)

name suggests for their large white tails which they flag behind them
as a warning signal when they are surprised and run for cover. The
white-tailed bucks also have a different variety of antler, with the tines
coming from one central beam that is curved forward. Mule deer
bucks have antlers that are bifurcated and branching in nature. Coyotes occasionally prey on sick, young, or old deer (as do domestic
dogs if left to roam unrestrained). The deer is the primary food source
for the mountain lion.

Elk, or wapiti, are more reclusive than mule deer and prefer areas
farther from the haunts of man, typically the most inaccessible
mountain country. They were originally a plains ungulate found
even in the eastern woodlands, but they have now retreated to the
highest mountains of the West. Locally they were hunted to extinction in the early twentieth century and then reintroduced. The elk is
considerably larger than the mule deer, weighing between 350 and
500 pounds. Its body is brownish grey with a chestnut mane on its

shoulders and neck, a white-yellow rump, and a short tail. The bulls grow antlers like the deer only much larger, sometimes weighing as much as 25 pounds each. The elk's musky scent is very powerful and unmistakable in the deep woods to those who are familiar with it. Elk tracks, like those of deer, are cloven and elongated and are generally twice as large, averaging four inches in length. The rut occurs in the early fall, usually in September, and the bulls make a peculiar high-pitched whistling sound as they challenge one another. At this time the bulls gather large harems of females, which they breed when not defending them from other bulls. Elk sign often encountered in the backcountry includes their large wallows, their droppings (often seen on the trails), and their enormous day beds, usually an oblong area of crushed grass five or six feet long. Elk are grazers, feeding primarily on grass, but they also feed on the brush as do mule deer. Like deer, elk migrate to lower terrain during the most severe period of the winter, but they may, again like deer, remain up high in years of below average snowfall.

Black bears, called by the Spanish *el oso negro*, are found throughout the Gila Wilderness. Doc Campbell reports that the largest black bear taken over the past 50 years to be in the 350-pound range, which is small for a mature black bear. The food chain here might not be as advantageous to black bears as it is farther north. Black bears are omnivorous, feeding on everything from ants and grasshoppers to grass and flowers to roots and berries to all forms of fresh and decayed meat. At different times of the year they feed in different micro-habitats and elevations. In the spring, for example, they are found in riparian woodlands and south-facing slopes, where their main food— green vegetation and winter-killed ungulates—is plentiful. The geographic concentration of bears at this time also facilitates the social contacts necessary for the mating process to occur which begins at this time. Later in the summer they are found at higher elevations, where they consume such diverse foods as small rodents, squirrel nut caches, bulbs, insects, and a great variety of plants. In the autumn the bears subsist on wild berries, trees, piñon nuts, prickly pear cactus fruit, and acorns. Bears return to these specific feeding areas year after year and seem to know when the various food sources found in them are ripe and ready. In the winter, the black bears hibernate in secluded areas, typically natural caves or dens excavated among trees, rocks, or under deadfall. The cubs are born in midwinter, usually twins, and stay with the sow the second winter in her den. Shy and secretive by nature, bears prefer remote side canyons, seldom-visited woodlands, and heavily forested slopes. Their familiar day beds, tracks, droppings, wallows, digs, feeding areas, and scratch trees can often be found by those who venture a few hundred yards from the trails. With the presence of man in the area, bears are largely nocturnal and rarely seen. The grizzly bear, called by the Spanish *el oso plateado*, is like the timber wolf now extinct from both New Mexico and Arizona. The closest remnant populations of both species are found in Chihuahua and Sonora, but experts predict both of these will soon be extinct, if they are not already. It is possible that both animals will one day be returned to the Gila Wilderness or to the Blue Range Primitive Area over the border in Arizona.

Mountain lions are found in good numbers in the Gila Wilderness Area, called by some puma or cougars. Adults are gray in body color, with a large tail, and usually weigh around 125 pounds. Their tracks are similar to those of a house cat only much larger. Even more retiring than black bears, lions are rarely if ever seen in the wild. They breed at any time of the year, the female bearing a litter of two or three kittens, which are tawny and black-spotted. Essentially a solitary breed of animal, the lion's individual range is quite large, averaging 20 square miles in mountainous country. Like other predators, they territorially mark trails, trees, and prominent boulders. Their cry is quite distinctive in the wilderness, like that of no other animal, and once heard, never forgotten. In areas too rugged for human hunters, the lions help keep the deer population within the carrying capacity of the range. Lions may also attack people.

Other important mammals of the Gila Wilderness include the coyote, the bobcat, the mink, the beaver, the fox, the badger, the weasel, the bat, the raccoon, the skunk, the rabbit, the porcupine, and a great variety of rodents from the wood rat to the pocket gopher to the tree squirrel. Probably the single most important mammal in the food chain in a magnitude completely out of proportion with its size is the field mouse, which feeds everything from rainbow trout and red-tailed hawks to skunks and black bears and breeds so prodigiously that this constant intense predation seems to have no effect on its population.

BIRDS.   A great variety of birds can be found in the Gila Wilderness from the tiny broad-tailed hummingbird that follows the sun south to Costa Rica every winter to the pine grouse that lives in the spruce-fir forests year-round. The terrestrial bird population can be divided into eight broad categories: air-insect, foilage-insect, foilage-seed or foilage-fruit, foilage-nectar, timber-search, ground-insect, ground-seed, and timber-drill. Along streams people frequently see the ouzel, or water dipper, fishing for small insects in the shallows. In the summer, many migratory songbirds inhabit these mountains, including the rosy finch, the solitary vireo, the goldfinch, the mountain bluebird, and various orioles and warblers, to name just a few of these ephemeral species. In cliff areas, the violet-green swallows are always fun to observe. The silence of the deep woods is often broken by the steady hammering of the downy woodpecker or by the hooting of the great horned owl. The cry of the raven is sometimes the only sound over a deep canyon at sunset, and on the high prairies the summer sun is always greeted as it rises from the eastern hills by the meadowlark. And of course no camp would be complete without its complement of Stellar's jays and common gray jays, the latter known affectionately to all wilderness travelers from Copper Canyon to the Yukon as the "Camp Robber." Finally, a great variety of water-loving birds is found in the Gila, including many species of ducks, geese, red-winged blackbirds, ospreys, kingfishers, and herons.

WILDFLOWERS.   The Gila has a great variety of wildflowers, ranging from those found most often in the Rocky Mountains, to those more typical of the Sonoran and Chihuahuan desert region. The flowers of the yucca, agave, and cactus species would fall in the latter category and are found most commonly at lower elevations with a southern exposure. At higher elevations, typical wildflowers are similar to those found in the Rockies: Indian paintbrush, shooting star, harebell, lupine, larkspur, and columbine, to name but a few. The first flowers in the spring include the pasque flower, the shooting star, the blue iris, the mariposa lily, and the white and purple violet. Summer sees a vast profusion of flowers, from the sacred datura of the canyon bottoms to the wild sunflowers of the grassy parks to the orchids of the high country. The last flowers of autumn include the purple aster, the blue gentian, cinquefoil, and other hardy species. Even in the early and late

Sunflowers abound in the Gila Wilderness. They are an important food source for birds, and their seeds were once eaten regularly by the Mogollon and Apache. (Photograph by John Murray)

winter, one can find the ubiquitous dandelion blooming somewhere in the low canyons, normally in proximity to a steaming hot spring.

TREES.   Typical trees found in the high mountains of the Gila Wilderness include the aspen (referred to by cowboys as "Quakers" because of the sound the leaves make in the wind), the blue spruce, the Engelmann's spruce, the Douglas fir, lodgepole pine, and ponderosa pine. The Douglas fir is an important commercial tree in the western

United States. Douglas fir grows second in size only to the California sequoia (giant sequoia and redwood), with heights of 200 feet or more and diameters of 3 to 6 feet. Under favorable conditions in the Pacific Northwest, specimens may live a thousand years, grow 10 feet through and 300 feet tall, with furrowed, cinnammon brown bark 1 foot thick. Douglas fir scatters its seeds prolifically (with over 30,000 seeds weighing only one pound) and young trees grow fast and dense in good soil. At 10 years they are 15 feet high, and in 25 years they are twice as tall, with sometimes as many as 1,000 trees to the acre. As they grow, the forest naturally thins in the competition. In a century the trees can reach 200 feet in height and may then number about 115 to the acre. In its smaller form, the Douglas fir, like the spruce, is prized for landscape planting and for Christmas trees. The wood, yellowish to light red in color, is strong for its fairly light weight and resistant to decay. The size of the tree permits the manufacture of lumber remarkably free of knots and other defects, with pieces up to 60 feet long and 2 feet square. The softwood veneer and plywood industries depend almost entirely on Douglas fir for raw materials. Recent new uses (fiberboard, book paper, wrapping paper) have been developed for sawmill leftovers. It is possible that the page on which this sentence is written was once part of a Douglas fir tree, a highly useful plant to our civilization, and one that, if properly managed in areas where it is harvested, will continue to serve us well.

Lower elevations in the Gila Wilderness support vast, almost ho-mogenous forests of ponderosa pine, which grows in every state west of the Great Plains, and is the state tree of Montana. It is second only to the Douglas fir in its continental distribution and reaches its max-imum growth in the Sierra forests of California, where it may live 500 years, attain heights exceeding 200 feet, and diameters of 5 to 8 feet. It may easily be distinguished from the Douglas fir or the piñon by its extremely long needles. During its early life, the ponderosa pine has dark brown, almost black, bark but as it grows the bark becomes plated and scaly, turning orange-yellow to cinnamon brown. The needles, some four to seven inches long, grow in clusters of three or sometimes two. The brown cones are clustered, too, standing erect on small stalks and growing three to six inches long. Like most pines, these cones require two seasons to mature. The ponderosa is the most valuable timber tree in the Southwest, ranging in a 300-mile belt from the Gila Wilderness northwest into the Kaibab Plateau of northern Arizona. It grows just above the sagebrush and piñon-juniper woodland, requiring less water than most other commercial trees. At its finest, the ponderosa pine rising to a broad, conical crown makes a stately and majestic tree. It provides a hard, strong, and fine-grained wood. High grade ponderosa is used for doors, sashes, frames, and paneling; low-grade wood for boxes, rafters, joists, and railroad ties.

Piñon and juniper are normally found in close association with one another, on midrange south-facing slopes, the piñon historically supplying natives with very palatable and nutritious nuts and the juniper producing edible berries. Interspersed with the piñon-juniper communities are Gambel's oak and Emory oak, both of which provide a rich crop of acorns in good years. Typical trees in the riparian communities include the cottonwood, willow, alder, sycamore, walnut, boxelder, with components of ponderosa pine and Douglas fir where conditions are favorable. These trees form thick deciduous woodlands in places, which are for the most part kept clear and parklike by seasonal flooding.

FISH.   The waters of the Gila Wilderness contain a great variety of fish, from the tiny minnows of the shallows to catfish, bass, suckers, and the large trout of the deep river pools. Rainbow trout are frequently stocked in the rivers and surrounding lakes. Brown trout and brook trout are found in Gila waters. Rainbow trout have the ability to leap when hooked and their spectacular gameness which results in hard fights, swift runs, and sudden leaps make them a favorite with anglers. Fishing in parts of the Gila, particularly the more remote waters of the West and Middle forks, can be very good in places at certain times of the year.

For the last eight years, the endangered Gila trout has been the subject of an intensive recovery effort. The interagency team consists of representatives from the New Mexico Game and Fish Department, the U.S. Fish and Wildlife Service, the U.S. Forest Service, and New Mexico State University. Gila trout have been reintroduced on Iron Creek and Little Creek and in Trail Canyon. Although presently still endangered, it is possible that one day limited catch on them might be permitted. Fishermen should check with rangers for protected waters, as well as for proper identification of this species.

A beautiful collared lizard, an abundant reptile in the Gila Wilderness, suns itself on a rock. (Photograph by John Murray)

REPTILES AND AMPHIBIANS. The Gila Wilderness is home for many reptiles and amphibians, ranging from the benign like the horned toad and the collared lizard to the deadly, like the coral snake and the diamondbacked rattlesnake. Most visitors encounter a species of reptile such as the bull snake, the box turtle, or the skink on their visit to the Wilderness. Frogs and toads are common near water. The Gila monster is extremely rare. Rattlesnakes are common below 9,000 feet and serve an extremely useful purpose in the ecosystem, helping to keep the constantly burgeoning rodent populations under control. The horned toad and bullfrog are protected species in the Gila Wilderness.

Geomorphology and Geography

The Gila Wilderness encompasses the headwaters of the Gila River, which drains south and west from the Mogollon Plateau through New Mexico and Arizona to its confluence with the Colorado River some 60 miles north of the Gulf of California. It is bounded on the north by the Plains of San Augustin and associated terrain; on the east by the Black Range; toward the south by the Pinos Altos Range; and toward the west by the Mogollon Rim. The greatest north-to-south distance through the Wilderness, as the crow flies, is approximately 27 miles, and, east to west, the longest distance is about 39 miles. Many geomorphic processes have been active in developing the surface features of the Gila Wilderness, including volcanism, faulting, and natural erosion. The most important force was a period of active volcanism about 65 million years ago. Prior to that time southwestern New Mexico was apparently part of an ancient scenario of warm tropical and semitropical seas and wet inland topography, which accounts for the many sedimentary rock formations (with fossils) which are now present in the region.

A second period of volcanic activity is thought to have occurred about 30 to 20 million years ago. It was during this period that two huge calderas were formed and then collapsed. Gila conglomerate, a thick blanket of sandstone, mudstone, and conglomerate, overlaps this volcanic layer in many parts of the Wilderness. Many of the canyon features—deeply eroded ash-flow tuff, for example—can be attributed to this ancient period. The flat mesas of the Gila uplands, formed by volcanic material ejected by these large shield volcanoes, were gradually eroded over the ages. A series of earthquakes also began to change the landscape through extensive faulting, producing areas of great vertical relief and generally north-to-south trending mountain ranges (such as the Mogollon Mountains). Some of these ranges are still slowly rising.

The Gila Wilderness and its environs have historically produced several valuable minerals, including gold and silver. The world famous "Bridal Chamber" of silver ore was located in Lake Valley. Other centers of mining included Kingston, in which there were once 27 separate mines, Mogollon, Hillsboro, Lake Valley, Mimbres,

Pinos Altos, and Silver City. One of the more unusual minerals found in the area is meerschaum (German for "seafoam"), a porous and extremely light clay material that can float in water when dry. Meerschaum was first discovered on Sapillo Creek in 1875 and was mined until about 1920, after an estimated two million pounds of the substance had been extracted.

PART 2.

THE HUMAN HISTORY

A brisk trot brought us to the base of the walls. . . . I was startled to see what appeared to be a one-storied house set in the face of the cliff, twenty or thirty feet above us. The walls were of flat stones set in some kind of mortar. A few small loop-holes appeared in the outer face, while the ends of rafters projected over the top.

> —from the journals of Lieutenant George Henry Sands, Sixth Cavalry, Fort Bayard, New Mexico, 1885, upon his discovery of the extensive cliff dwellings now included in the Gila Cliff Dwellings National Monument

Pre-Mogollon History

Long before Columbus and Coronado there were people living in southwestern New Mexico. Of these first Americans, not much is known. Much of their culture was as perishable as the grasses on which they walked and the game they hunted. Only a few sites have been found. The first period of human inhabitation in the Southwest is known as the Paleo-Indian period, represented successively by the Clovis, Folsom, and Cody complexes in New Mexico. Their adaptations to the environment include gathering in the uplands and big-game hunting at the lower elevations and persist from earliest times to around 5500 B.C. Hunting in organized groups with flint and bone-tipped weapons, including the atlatl (spear thrower) and spear, the Paleo-Indians were regularly able to ambush and kill large animals. As the climate became drier and hunting became less profitable, these people began to turn to foraging and gathering.

Early Archaic cultures (sometimes referred to as the Desert Culture) began to arise after the Paleo-Indian period. They were more adapted to an arid or semiarid environment. An understanding of the Archaic period is also hampered by a paucity of excavated sites. It has been suggested by some authorities that by as early as 4800 B.C. the Southwest was occupied by several different interacting groups, sometimes referred to as the Elementary Southwestern Culture. This is probably the first time that the Southwest may be considered a separate and distinct cultural unit. By around 3000 B.C., or possibly earlier, the earliest materials of what anthropologists call the Sulphur Springs Stage of the "Cochise Period" (a tool tradition) had begun to emerge. Excavations at this level suggest a mixed foraging economy. Baskets were used for gathering, and milling slabs and cobble manos were used to process natural food sources. Using modern foragers as analogues, scientists postulate a small band of around 50 persons as the basic societal unit.

Between 1800 B.C. and 1500 B.C. a primitive variety of maize, or corn, was introduced into the southern Southwest from Mexico. It gradually spread through all but possibly the western sector. In the Cochise area, this maize was accompanied by domestic squash. The eventual development of small seasonal surpluses may have been important in the seasonal aggregation of populations and to a slightly more sedentary way of life. There is some evidence to suggest that by 1500 B.C. to 1000 B.C. a significant change in the previous foraging pattern occurred. Between 1000 B.C. and 500 B.C. an even more vigorous strain of corn reached the area from the south, as well as the red kidney bean. Both are excellent sources of protein.

The Mogollon

During the Christian Era three major cultural regions began to arise in the Southwest: the Anasazi, the Hohokam, and the Mogollon. All but the Anasazi are thought to have evolved from the more widespread Cochise Culture, which in turn developed from the even more ancient Desert Culture. The Mogollon were located in southwestern New Mexico and southeastern Arizona and are named for the rugged mountains which lie roughly in the center of their area. The Mogollon are commonly divided into six smaller geographic groups. As with the Anasazi and Hohokam cultures, the Mogollon have also been subdivided into time periods. One tentative classification divides the culture into five time periods, ranging from 300 B.C. to approximately A.D. 1250. Most Mogollons inhabited mountainous areas, but some lived in the lower transitional areas. Early Mogollon sites were located well back from the mainstream of travel, on ridgetops and near the edges of mesas. Later Mogollon sites (after A.D. 500 to A.D. 600) tended to increase in number and to be located in more accessible areas, such as in valleys near streams or rivers where agriculture and irrigation could be carried out.

The earliest Mogollon dwellings were large pithouses with storage pits excavated into the floors. The houses within each village were not arranged in any pattern, and the number ranged from a few to more than 50. Pithouses came into vogue in northeastern Europe around 25,000 years ago and have been found across Europe, in northern Asia through Siberia, and in Alaska. Mogollon pithouses range in size from around 150 square feet to about 1,089 square feet. All of them until around A.D. 900 are roundish, bean-shaped, ovoid, or D-shaped. In later times, they were quadrangular and generally smaller, less than 500 square feet. Many interesting cultural items have been excavated from these sites.

Around the year A.D. 1000 a significant change took place among the Mogollon, a change seen both in the pottery and in the architecture. In the pottery, the red-on-whites and red-on-browns were completely replaced by a black-on-white type that, while locally made, was possibly inspired by Anasazi types north of the Mogollon area. A greater variety of shapes is also found, including pitchers, jars, ladles,

The Gila Cliff Dwellings, as seen from inside the main arch of the key structure in the National Monument. (Photograph by Charles William Murray, Junior)

effigy shapes, and eccentric shapes. The most extraordinary black-on-white pottery to have developed was Mimbres Bold Face and Mimbres Classic black-on-white, whose designs are not only geometric but also naturalistic, depicting animals, fish, humans, insects, and composite creatures. One author has written that no prehistoric southwestern pottery can compare with Mimbres Classic "in its expression of the beauty and vitality of life and nature." After A.D. 1100 or perhaps before, experimenting included polychrome pottery with designs executed in black and white paints on a red background. In the architecture, the possible Anasazi influence can be seen in the Gila Cliff Dwellings at the eastern entrance to the Gila Wilderness.

Sometime in the early 1300s the Mogollon people suddenly left the area. It is not known why this occurred. Some authorities theorize they joined other Indians to the north or south. One theory has them moving closer to the Rio Grande and working with new pottery and architectural styles, the ancestors of the historic Piro Indians south of

Belen, New Mexico. Others speculate that their numbers increased, through birth and immigration, to a point beyond the carrying capacity of the area and that the culture then collapsed. Still others conjecture that the Mogollon fell victim to disease, drought, or war, or a combination of these factors. For whatever reason, they were gone by A.D. 1400 when the last wave of Asian immigrants entered the areas from the north, people destined to form two distinct modern tribes: the Apache and the Navajo.

The Apache

The Chiricahua Apache ranged throughout southwestern New Mexico, southeastern Arizona, and northern Sonora and Chihuahua. When they were first encountered by the Spanish in 1541 the Apache were apparently a peaceful and nomadic people, pursuing a hunter/gatherer way of life. Coronado's men reported that, after reaching a pass in southeastern Arizona they called Chichiticale (possibly Apache Pass), they passed into the country of a nomadic people who lived in rancherias (possibly the Apache wickiup, a dwelling made of branches and animal hides). Shortly after 1600 Spanish documents begin to indicate a concern over Apache depredations. As the Apache acquired the horse, probably by the late 1600s, their mobility and the extent of their raiding pattern increased. By 1700 the Apache were firmly entrenched in their range and were well organized from a military standpoint, a dramatic change from their previous hunter/gatherer state. As Spanish settlements increased in the area, moving northward through the Santa Cruz River Valley in Arizona and the Rio Grande Valley in New Mexico, conflicts between the two groups increased.

Many local ranches, towns, missions, and small mining stakes suffered heavily from Apache raids in the eighteenth century. Despite a presidio, or military garrison, policy across the northern frontier, little progress was made in diminishing the Apache threat in this period. Also ineffective were sporadic civilian forces gathered for punitive actions. Gradually, the policy of capturing Apaches and using them as slaves and of paying professional killers for Apache scalps came into being. By 1767 the Jesuits were expelled from the New World colonies, partly because of their attempts to moderate some of these secular policies. Scalp bounty laws were passed in 1835 in Sonora and in 1837 in Chihuahua. Many of these bounty hunters operated in southwestern New Mexico, including the area now known as the Gila Wilderness Area.

One of the most infamous incidents occurred near the Santa Rita copper mines, south of the Gila Wilderness Area, in 1837. Of the two major accounts, the bloodiest and least likely is related by frontiersman John Cremony, who heard it years later. The version by a Mr.

Wilson, who later became the first mayor of Los Angeles, is probably more accurate. He was camped nearby and obtained his facts from eyewitnesses. According to Wilson, Juan Jose Compa, a Mimbres Apache chieftain who had been educated by the Spanish and who had studied for the priesthood, brought his tribe to the vicinity of the mines at the invitation of James Johnson, an American trapper and part-time scalp hunter in Sonora. Johnson and Juan Jose had apparently been good friends up to this point. Unbeknownst to Juan Jose, however, Johnson had accepted a large bounty from the governor of Sonora for Juan Jose's scalp. After the festivities began, Johnson fired a small cannon into the crowd of Apaches, killing and wounding many of them. An accomplice of Johnson's named Gleason shot and wounded Juan Jose, who called out for Johnson's assistance. Johnson walked over and shot Juan Jose dead. Among the Apaches who survived this betrayal was Mangas Coloradas (literally "red sleeves"), an astute leader destined to become an important chief. For a period after this incident, until Mangas Coloradas ordered a halt, there were a number of reprisal raids on American trappers, explorers, and settlers in the Black Range and Gila Wilderness region.

A young member of Mangas Coloradas's tribe at this time was Goyathlay (later named Geronimo at the battle of Arispe in Sonora), who was born, by his own account, in the year 1829 (the date is probably incorrect) somewhere "around the headwaters of the Gila River," and who was also fated to play a powerful role in Southwestern history. Geronimo, together the Mangas Coloradas and Victorio, would later form a powerful triumvirate that would resist American expansion and colonization until Geronimo's ultimate surrender in September 1886. Cochise, the hereditary chieftain of the western band of the Chiricahua Apache, controlled the lands of southeastern Arizona, including the strategic area known as Apache Pass (southeast of present day Wilcox, Arizona).

The war between Mexico and the United States broke out in 1846. By 1848 the war was over, and the treaty of Guadalupe Hidalgo signed that year, conjoined with the Gadsden Purchase (1854), brought the whole of the Southwest into the domain of America. According to the terms of the treaty, the Spanish residing in the area were allowed to remain on their original land grants. In July 1850, under the provisions of the Compromise of 1850, California entered the Union as a free state. Almost immediately in their quest for the rich gold fields of the Sacramento Valley discovered in 1848, more and more Americans began to travel through the Southwest. The conventional route, which has since become known as the California Trail, led west from El Paso across southern New Mexico, crossing Stein's Pass near the border with Arizona, and Apache Pass near the north end of the Chiricahua Mountains. In 1851 John Bartlett led a surveying crew through southwestern New Mexico for the United States Boundary Commission and met and held counsel with both Geronimo and Mangas Coloradas. Bartlett established his headquarters near the Santa Rita copper mines, which had been all but abandoned by the Mexicans after 1838, and renamed the facility Ft. Webster.

The uneasy truce between the Apache leaders and the Americans ended in the spring of 1858 with the "Dad" Evans incident. "Dad" Evans, together with more than 100 prospectors, arrived in the area of Pinos Altos, New Mexico, in the winter of 1857–58, following the discovery of gold there the preceding year. They camped directly in the middle of the deer hunting grounds used by Mangas Coloradas and his second-in-command Victorio. An incident arose over trespassing and Mangas Coloradas was bound to a pine tree and whipped with a heavy leather harness strap. In the weeks that followed, over forty Americans were killed in the Gila country and its environs by Apaches.

On February 3, 1861, Lt. George Bascom was sent to Apache Pass to recover a captive boy believed stolen and held by Cochise. Cochise denied the charges. Further misunderstandings ensued and Cochise and his family were taken prisoner and held by Bascom's small force near Apache Pass. Cochise managed to escape and raise a large Apache force. Americans were killed, including hostages taken by Cochise, who demanded his family be released. In retaliation, Bascom ordered three members of Cochise's family hanged on a small hill outside his camp. At this point a state of war existed between the Apache and the Americans in the region, a condition that would not change until General O.O. Howard's courageous peace mission to Cochise in 1872. By the summer of 1861 terror reigned supreme in southwestern New Mexico and southeastern Arizona. The only secure places were a

The fruit of the prickly pear cactus, shown here in flower, was an important food source for the Apache. (Photograph by John Murray)

few cities, army posts, fortified mines, and heavily secured ranch houses. On September 27, 1861, Cochise, Mangas Coloradas, and several hundred warriors made a daring daylight raid on Pinos Altos, but withdrew when Confederate Arizona Guards appeared. As the South took the early lead in the Civil War, the Union withdrew from Forts Buchanan and Breckenridge. For a brief time the Apache rejoiced, believing they had at last chased the bluecoats from the desert. Soon, however, the Union returned, and, after suffering a great defeat at the Battle of Apache Pass on July 15, 1862, the Apache returned to the time-honored tactics of guerrilla warfare. On January 13, 1863, Mangas Coloradas was killed by soldiers while in custody at Ft. Bayard near Pinos Altos, thus effectively removing one of the important Apache leaders.

In his recollections the early pioneer Jack Stockbridge recorded several incidents involving the Apache Indians that occurred in the 1860s in the Gila country. The first occurred in either 1863 or 1864 and was told to Stockbridge by Noah Owens, who was then stationed at Fort West on the Gila River. As Owens related to Stockbridge some years later in Raton, New Mexico, one day a man of about 60 years of age and a younger man of around 20 came into the fort on horseback from the mountains farther up the Gila. They were the sole survivors of a party attacked by Apaches in the Wilderness. After the attack they had ridden past the Gila Hot Springs into the big canyon of the Gila but found it boxed up and full of quicksand. They turned off the north side and rode west until they dropped off into Turkey Creek Canyon; camping at the Turkey Creek Hot Springs. The next morning the old man found signs of gold while out looking for the horses. The two then followed Turkey Creek to the Gila River and took it down to Fort West. After remaining at Fort West for several days to rest and shoe their horses, the two left the area to winter in Tucson. The next spring they returned and against warnings from the army rode back into the Gila Wilderness. Their military escort left them at the mouth of Skeleton Canyon. Just as the soldiers turned back, they heard shooting. In the short time that had elapsed, both men had been killed by the Apaches.

The next year, again according to Stockbridge, old Fort West was closed, but Fort Bayard at Pinos Altos remained in operation. Three soldiers attached to the Eighth Cavalry at Fort Bayard under the guidance of a soldier named Sidman went prospecting for gold up Turkey Creek near the confluence with Manzanita Creek. About a week or ten days after leaving Fort Bayard, Sidman returned without his companions, saying they had been killed by Apaches near Turkey Creek. Sidman was suspected of killing his companions himself and then blaming it on the Apaches. According to Stockbridge, he continued to prospect and work small mines in the Gila country, including a claim on Mogollon Creek. Apparently some of the ore he brought out was fairly high grade, in one case bringing $4,600 for 150 pounds of it. Years later, Stockbridge relates that a man camped on Turkey Creek across from the mouth of Miller Spring Canyon found three skeletons while digging under a big overhanging bluff. Stockbridge suggests these may have been Sidman's three missing companions of the mid-1860s, whose story unfortunately died with them.

In his book *Black Range Tales*, James McKenna tells many stories of the Apache period in southwestern New Mexico. One of them concerns a civilian posse that was formed in Silver city in 1870. After sustaining numerous depredations, particularly on the road between Silver City and Pinos Altos, the local residents decided, in McKenna's words, "to teach the Indians a needed lesson". A meeting was held and it was decided to follow the local Apaches to their winter camp among the San Francisco Mountains near Clifton, Arizona. John Bullard, one of the founders of Silver City, was elected the leader of the party. Their trail took them along Bear Creek from Pinos Altos, westward to the Gila River, up Duck Creek Valley, across Cactus Flats, and over the divide to the Gila Hot Springs, where the party stopped their second night out from Silver City. The next morning they headed up the West Fork of the Gila River. Snow began to fall, and it was difficult to track the Indians. Suddenly the scouts wheeled around and signaled Bullard that they had sighted the Apache encampment. Within minutes, Bullard had divided his company into three groups: one to guard the packtrain, a second to attack from the south, and a third to attack from the north. Taken by surprise, the Apaches were overwhelmed. Bullard went forward on foot to strip the dead of their arms and was shot in the chest by an Apache who had feigned death. A wagon was brought from Silver City to the Hot Springs and Bullard's body was returned to Silver City where he was buried with full military honors. The day after the fight a cowboy found an infant child still alive near his dead Apache mother. The child was given to foster parents in Silver City who later gave the boy to Apache parents on the San Carlos Reservation.

In 1868 the Chiricahua Apache were moved to the Ojo Caliente reservation in Grant County near the north end of the Black Range. Despite the watchfulness of reservation officials, small bands occasionally slipped away from the reservation to harass local prospectors and ranchers. Settlers complained and, against the wishes of both Apaches and Army officers, the Indians were marched to the San Carlos Reservation in Arizona. In 1874 Cochise died in Arizona. Victorio was the leader of the Chiricahuas in southwestern New Mexico at the time. Twice he fled from the San Carlos Reservation, only to be returned by the army. His final escape occurred on September 4, 1879, during which he took with him a small army of Chiricahua and Mescalero Apaches, as well as some southern Apaches and Comanches. His force numbered over 350 warriors. He immediately set out from his stronghold in the Black Range, near the headwaters of the Animas River, 20 miles above Hillsboro and 40 miles south of Ojo Caliente. Along the way the warriors attacked Company E, Ninth Cavalry at their encampment, killing 5 soldiers and 3 civilians and stealing 46 horses. Commands from west Texas to central Arizona were put on highest alert, and troops gathered for what was to be a 13-month hunt.

On September 18, 1879, Victorio prepared a skillful ambush for the men of the Ninth Cavalry. Near Hillsboro, Captains Byers and Dawson found themselves pinned down at the bottom of a rocky defile and suffered serious casualties. The fighting continued all day. At one point, Second Lieutenant Matthias W. Day rescued and bore off a wounded soldier across 200 yards of open ground, every space of it under heavy fire. His commanding officer, Captain Byers, later threatened to courtmartial Day for refusing to obey a direct order "to retreat and leave his wounded behind."

Upon review at higher command, Second Lieutenant Day was instead awarded the Congressional Medal of Honor. By the end of the day, 8 soldiers were dead, 2 seriously wounded, and 53 horses and mules had been abandoned in the field.

Four days later, Lieutenants Blocksom and Gatewood, dispatched from Fort Bayard to assist Byers and Dawson, were similarly engaged by Victorio and had several soldiers in their command killed. On October 7, 1879, contact was made with Victorio's central camp. Major Morrow of the Ninth Cavalry attacked the encampment and made off with numerous horses and mules. On October 13, 1879, a vigilante force of volunteers from Mesilla entered the Black Range in search of Victorio. They, like the others before, rode directly into an Apache ambush. Six were killed.

Feeling too pressured in the Black Range, Victorio faded south into the Florida Mountains. On October 27, 1879, hot on Victorio's trail, Lieutenant Gatewood and his small force were ambushed near a desert spring in the Guzman Mountains and repelled a brutal Apache attack in the middle of the night. Battles continued on both sides of the border for many months. Finally, deep in Mexico, Mexican troops overtook and surrounded Victorio's band. On October 14, 1880, in the Tres Castillos Hills some 92 miles north of Chihuahua City, Victorio and his warriors fought their last battle. Victorio, repeatedly wounded in the action, was killed by a Tarahumari scout, Maruicio, who was later presented a nickle-plated rifle by the Mexican government in addition to the reward money. During the fight, some 78 Apache warriors were killed. Around 68 women and children were captured, as well as approximately 200 horses and mules. Nana escaped with 30 warriors, but later surrendered with Geronimo.

After the death of Victorio, the only major Apache leader left in the field was Geronimo, who with Naiche, the son of Cochise, continued to lead the tribe both on and off the San Carlos Reservation. During this period, Geronimo frequently sought refuge in the vastness of the Gila Wilderness, as well as in the Chiricahua Mountains and the Sierra Madre Mountains. In his recollections, Jack Stockbridge relates that one of the last battles occurred at Soldier Hill near the Meader Ranch on Big Dry Creek in December 1885. Geronimo ambushed the troops who were pursuing him at this location and then fled up a long narrow ridge of Baldy Mountain onto the west slope of the Mogollon Mountains. The cavalry regrouped and followed Geronimo's trail. Finding unscalable cliffs, they decided Geronimo must have come down Mogollon Creek. The west fork of the Mogollon is on one side of the ridge and the main Mogollon Creek to the south of the ridge. What the soldiers didn't realize is that Geronimo had gone around the cliffs, come down the ridge from farther up, and then gone into a little canyon that runs into Tepee Canyon. Here there was a good spring at the head of the canyon within a hundred feet of the ridge. With the narrow ridge closed by snows in the winter, it made a natural fortress. Here Geronimo made his secret camp during the winter of 1885–86, his last season of freedom in the Wilderness. Stockbridge relates that when he visited the site in 1900, he could still see evidence of the camp: "It looked like they had been there for a year. There was piles of wood chopped up and several pretty good-sized trees cut down with logs laid so that they could put canvas over them."

Montague Stevens, a British rancher who had extensive holdings in the western foothills of the Mogollon Mountains, had constant problems with the Apaches led by Geronimo prior to his surrender. In his recollections, he relates that in the early spring of 1885 a former Cambridge classmate of his, E. W. Lyon, came out to visit him at his ranch. On May 21, Lyon offered to ride down to Alma where Stevens had his mail delivered once a week. After learning that Geronimo had escaped again from San Carlos, Stevens, his foreman, and six or eight others started down the trail to Alma, fearing that Lyon might be ambushed by the Apaches. Finding scraps of blue paper on the trail, Stevens and the others conducted a close search and shortly found Lyon's body, shot through the heart. Stockbridge tells of several others killed in the Gila Wilderness during the 1880s, including Sergeant James Cooney on Mineral Creek, Prior and Lilley, and Papanoe, Wood, and Poland. Finally, on September 3, 1886, Geronimo and Naiche surrendered in Skeleton Canyon, just north of the Mexican border in the extreme southeastern corner of Arizona. Accepting the surrender was Lieutenant Gatewood and General Miles, a Medal of Honor winner from the Civil War and the last American officer to accept the surrender of a hostile American Indian tribe. The Apache wars were at last over and relative peace and tranquility reigned over Apacheria. A few Apaches lived on in Sonora and Chihuahua, sporadically attacking Mormon settlers there until they too disappeared by the turn of the century. In his recollections, the wilderness ranger Henry Woodrow records that after the surrender there was one last Apache who continued to live in the Mogollons with his wife and two or three children. Part of the time he apparently camped at the head of Mogollon Creek and Turkey Creek. Once while out exploring with William "Horn Silver Bill" Dorsey of Silver City, Woodrow came upon these Indians. He and Dorsey were riding up a rough side canyon at the head of Mogollon Creek. The Indians saw them and ran off behind some large rocks. Woodrow and Dorsey turned back the other way. This was in 1900, and by Woodrow's account these were the last Apache to reside in what is today the Gila Wilderness. He further reports that the old chief was finally killed at the north end of the Black Range and his wife sent to the San Carlos Reservation in Arizona. The Apache were gone, but the history they made would endure. Even today, our Gila Wilderness place names reflect their era: Lookout Mountain, named for its use as a lookout point for Geronimo; Lilley Mountain, named for an individual killed by Apaches; and Apache Creek, named for the tribe that once made their home here, to cite just a few.

THE AMERICANS

The large influx of Americans into the Gila country during the last quarter of the nineteenth century dramatically impacted the land, with both flora and fauna affected by the overuse of resources. Timber was clear-cut to fuel mines, build homes, heat homes, and accommodate the needs of large numbers of army troops. There was wholesale overgrazing in areas, with the denuding of vegetation resulting in severe flooding by the early 1890s. Game, once common, began to diminish. Species became threatened with extirpation, such as the gray wolf, grizzly bear, Merriam's elk, bighorn sheep, and river otter. Alarmed by this situation, President McKinley formed the Gila River Forest Reserve on March 2, 1899, permanently withdrawing the lands from settlement and preserving them from further development. In 1903 the first scientific examination was made by the U.S. Geological Survey which recommended the careful supervision and management of the forest and grasslands so as to avoid destruction by ranchers and settlers.

The next administrative move came in 1907 when the Gila River Forest Reserve was placed under the newly created Forest Service. By 1909 the Gila had been divided into districts and management had begun in earnest. In 1909 Henry Woodrow became a forest guard in the Wilderness; he soon became a district ranger and held this position until 1942 when he retired. His primary responsibility was to fight fires and enforce Forest Service regulations pertaining to grazing. In addition he had to build and clear trails, supervise two Forest Service trapper/hunters, make out reports on pastures not under permit, assist in the survey of various homestead claims made on the Middle Fork under the Forest Homestead Act of June 11, 1906, measure cordwood at wood sales, and post Forest Service boundaries. Other major projects in the early years included the construction of a ranger station at White Creek by Woodrow himself (there was little money for contract work in those days), the construction of a telephone line from Little Dry Creek Ranger Station to Center Baldy in 1914, and the introduction of 19,500 sheep into the district in 1913. On January 6, 1912 New Mexico became a state. The first wooden tower for a fire lookout in the district was built in 1917 on Granite Peak. By 1920, dynamite was furnished to trail crews, and in 1921 a house was built on the top of the old tower on Mogollon Baldy. Modern times had come to the Gila.

By the 1920s, overgrazing was recognized as a serious problem. Grazing management was changed to better protect the land and the fragile watersheds. In 1925, a northern elk species was released to replace the extinct Merriam's elk. These elk have since flourished and now number in the thousands. About this same time, the grizzly bear, timber wolf, and bighorn sheep all vanished from the Gila. The last river otter was trapped in 1953. Various issues of the time appeared in *The Gila Monster*, a newsletter put out by Gila National Forest personnel on their personal time, reflecting their concern with the declining environment of the forest. It was during this period back in Washington that the forester Aldo Leopold fought for and obtained wilderness designation for what is now the Gila Wilderness. The Gila Wilderness, originally containing around 755,000 acres, was designated in 1924. It was the first such wild area to be so preserved in the world. The wilderness concept itself was largely invented by Leopold, an assistant district forester in the regional office at Albuquerque. Following this precedent other areas were established throughout America. During the 1930s, another forester, Bob Marshall, worked hard to create a national system of wilderness areas. In 1936, Civilian Conservation Corps labor was used in the district to do much of the work that had previously been left undone due to underfunding, a chronic problem for the Forest Service then and now. Also an annual Trail Ride was begun by the Wilderness Society in cooperation with the Forest Service. These continued for 24 years. The year 1938 was known as the "Earthquake Year." Earthquakes started in August and continued through the fall, resulting in additional work for trail crews from damaging slides. Woodrow reports in his *History of the McKenna Park District* that 1941 was a year of abnormally high snowfall and rainfall, resulting in the worst flooding since 1904. Once again, trail crews had their work cut out for them, repairing damage to trails all over the mountains. By World War II, U.S. Forest Service "smoke jumpers" had so perfected the skill of parachuting into wildfire areas that they were recruited to train the first paratroopers to fight in Europe.

Since the 1924 designation of the Gila Wilderness, several major changes have occurred. In 1933 the administration of the Gila Cliff Dwellings was transferred to the National Park Service. Also that year the North Star Mesa Road was built to give access to the Beaver-head District and the eastern division was named the Black Range Primitive Area. In 1944 the Gila Wilderness Boundary was drawn away from a little over 5,000 acres in the southwest corner. This allowed for the mining of flourite, an important mineral in the man-ufacture of steel for the war effort. In 1957 boundaries were also redrawn to allow a road to the Gila Cliff Dwellings. The area to the east of the road corridor was designated the Gila Primitive Area and that to the west the Gila Wilderness Area. In the late 1960s, a paved road was put in to allow increased access. More recently the area formerly designated as the Gila Primitive Area has been restored to the wilderness status it formerly enjoyed. Since 1967 managers have noticed that flooding has been getting worse in the Gila country. It is thought improvements and adjustments in fire policy will correct this problem, which has possibly resulted from the combined effects of both overgrazing and lack of fire. Ground litter provided by dense fire-protected pines is poor. Water tends to rapidly run off. Grasses and shrubs, on the other hand, offer better moisture retention which is less likely to produce serious flooding. Two hundred-year level floods in 1984–85, which led to the area being declared a federal disaster area, destroyed many trails and roads in the Gila region. Emergency relief provided by the federal government has led to the reconstruction of many trails and roads. River crossings in the canyon bottoms are being restored, and trails are being brought out of the floodplain onto the sides of the canyon where possible. Large cairns are being built in places to mark the route of travel. It is hoped that the use of a natural fire policy together with preplanned ignition in some cases will permit a more natural role for fire in the Wilderness. Fires will help to clear out old stands and encourage secondary growth, which should increase moisture retention thus decreasing flooding. Also regular fires will avoid a fuel load buildup which carries with it the risk of a catastrophic fire.

The concept of the wilderness area, as first founded in the Gila, is one of the significant accomplishments of the American people in this century and will no doubt rank among its finest contributions to posterity. Ideally, in the years to come humankind's presence will

Today's hikes and horse trips into the Gila are tomorrow's history. Pictured here is the author's father, Charles W. Murray, Junior, on the August 1987 trip told in the Epilogue. (Photograph by John Murray)

continue to be held to a minimum and the forces of nature allowed to work unencumbered by our interference. Perhaps one day we will see the restoration of other endangered species to the Gila Wilderness, recoveries that will be as successful as that for the Gila trout. The grizzly bear could probably make its home in these mountains again, as could the river otter and possibly the Mexican wolf (now confined to captive breeding programs). Finally, it is to be hoped that the restoration of natural fire conditions to the Gila Wilderness will permit the restoration of historic vegetative patterns.

Part 3.

Backcountry Travel

That night we reached a point where the [Gila] river forked, and encamped on the point between the forks. We found here a boiling spring so near the main stream, that the fish caught in one might be thrown into the other. In six minutes it would be thoroughly cooked.

—James O. Pattie, *Personal Narrative* (1831)

WEATHER

The weather in the Gila Wilderness is typical of that found in the desert uplands of the Southwest. Precipitation varies from 12 inches in the lower regions to over 20 inches in the higher elevations. Most of this precipitation occurs either as snowfall in the winter months or as rain in the late summer, from the second week in July through early September. Winters are usually cold at night on all parts of the Gila. Lower elevations and south-facing slopes will cool down to about 20 degrees Fahrenheit, but at 7,000 feet and higher temperatures may drop to 0 degrees or lower. During the day in the direct sunlight temperatures at all these elevations may rise to 65 degrees or more. Summer temperatures in the 90s are common up to 6,000 feet during the day, but generally at night it cools off into the low 60s. Higher elevations generally see daytime highs in the 70s and 80s, with night-time temperatures dropping off to 45 degrees or so. Extremely hot weather such as is encountered in the low desert is rarely encountered in this mountainous area. Afternoon or evening thunderstorms occur frequently from mid-July through early September. These storms are normally of short duration, but can be intense at times and yield heavy rain, causing flash floods in the canyons. Drought is common at the lower elevations in the semidesert portions of the Gila Wilderness. Plants often suffer stress from lack of moisture in the early spring and fall, and, in every ten-year period, normally two or three of these years will be deficient in summer and winter moisture. Frost can occur even during the summer in some of the higher canyons and on some of the higher ridges above 8,000 feet. In summary, the climate of the Gila country is continental in character with Pacific air masses entering the range from the west, particularly during the winter, and Gulf air masses from the southeast, particularly during the summer. It is not as severe as that found in the Rockies to the north or in the Sonoran and Chihuahuan deserts to the south and probably for that reason is a popular area to visit.

MARCH AND APRIL. The Winter is normally over by mid- to late March at lower and middle elevations in the Gila Wilderness Area. Mild winters have seen the higher trails open, though not always in

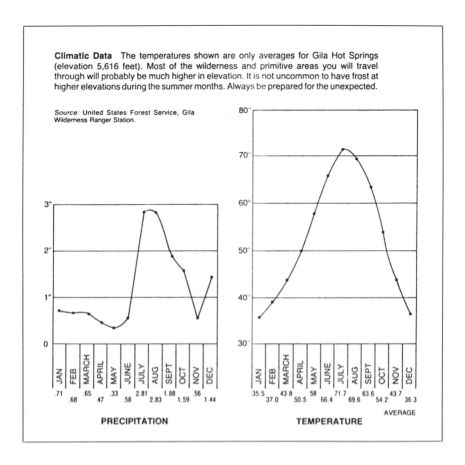

Climatic Data The temperatures shown are only averages for Gila Hot Springs (elevation 5,616 feet). Most of the wilderness and primitive areas you will travel through will probably be much higher in elevation. It is not uncommon to have frost at higher elevations during the summer months. Always be prepared for the unexpected.

Source: United States Forest Service, Gila Wilderness Ranger Station.

PRECIPITATION

TEMPERATURE

fine shape, by April. After hard winters, it has been difficult to get above 10,000 feet until June. High water on the rivers can be an obstacle to travel during the spring runoff, which usually reaches its peak during the last week in March and the first week in April. As the rivers drain the snowfall of the preceding winter, they briefly swell to three or four times their average seasonal flow and attract flotillas of river rafters. This period is also a time of fairly low precipitation and mild weather, with daytime highs reaching into the 70s and nighttime lows dropping only into the 30s or possibly the 20s. Snowfall is rare, but now unknown. At lower elevations the spring wildflowers are at their best: the pasque flower, mariposa lily, yellow violet, spring beauty, sand lily, and ubiquitous dandelion. The new grass appears on the canyon floors and in the ponderosa forests, and the deer and elk begin to graze upcountry from their winter range. Trees and bushes begin to bud and sprout their first leaves and the songbirds start to arrive: the robin, meadowlark, vireo, goldfinch, and mountain blue-bird. Frogs chant from the swollen riverbanks and on warm days the garter snakes are often startled on the trail as they lie out in the sun. In some dark canyon far from man the black bear sow and her two new cubs emerge from their winter den, and, in a rocky whelping den near some grassy park, the coyote pups are fed their first grasshoppers and mice. The summer stars begin to show themselves a little in the night sky, and everywhere the promise of the summer's coming bounty is seen. Best of all, the crowds are still far away, and except for spring break week the popular trails are often dry and nearly deserted at this time of the year.

MAY AND JUNE.   May and June are two of the more popular months to visit the Gila, after the spring runoff and before the summer heat and flash flood seasons. Fishing can be good to excellent on many of the streams and rivers as the trout are stirred to activity by the long sunny days, warm water, and renewed profusion of aquatic life. Many of the trails leading into the higher elevations open up during this period, though snow may be found in places and after a hard winter may still block hikers. The canyon woodlands are dark green by June, and at lower elevations the first wildflowers of summer begin to appear: the prickly pear cactus, purple pea vine, and sacred datura. Wild strawberries can be found in places. The birds have all returned by late May and with them the bees and butterflies of sum-mer. The deer fawns and elk calves are born in remote areas, and the herds begin to settle on their summer range high in the mountains. The aspen groves are green by June and their leaves begin to make the soft quaking sound that for many is synonymous with summer in the Gila high country. Days are long now and often hot, with tempera-tures climbing into the low 80s or even 90s at the lower elevations. Nights are still cool, as they almost always are in the desert uplands. It is a good time of the year to rent some horses and pack into a remote fishing hole or head up into the Mogollons to see how far you can get before you reach the last of the snow.

JULY AND AUGUST.   July is the warmest month of the year in the Gila, and, as the days get hotter, people naturally seem to drift higher into the mountains. Here they will find the summer wildflowers at their very best: the columbine, lupine, larkspur, harebell, orchids, and bluebells. All parts of the Gila are dry and accessible to foot or horse travel now, and the Mogollons are at the peak of their beauty with the ferns sometimes stirrup-deep in the forest and the grass in the parks reaching over your knees. The maximum biomass for the ecosystem is reached in July shortly after the longest day of the year. Biomass is the living weight of a region, that is, the amount of organic matter produced by photosynthesis usually expressed in calories or grams per meter. Naturally this varies by altitude and latitude and usually culminates after the summer solstice. July and August are months of increased rainfall. In fact, most of the precipitation for parts of the Gila country occurs during this period. Always pack a poncho and be prepared to avoid the canyons and remain on high ground if rangers warn of flash flood conditions or if other conditions warrant this action. The Gila high country is a good place to go in the late summer to escape the heat of the lower desert if you live in such an area. The Perseid meteor shower is always a favorite in early August.

SEPTEMBER AND OCTOBER.   For many, autumn is the only time to visit the Gila. The hardwood leaves are changing, the aspen are turning bright yellow, the elk are bugling, and the trout fishing is good again after the slow days of summer. The trails are drier than summer, and the canyons are safer. The nut crop—piñon, acorn, and walnut—is ripe for picking, and, if you tire of this, the berry crop is usually good as well—raspberries, wild grapes, chokecherry. The fruit of the man-zanita and prickly pear cactus are found in abundance. The flowers begin to dwindle as the days shorten and the nights become cooler until only the purple aster remains, blooming defiantly until it is finally buried in the snow. In the autumn, the Gila Wilderness is a favorite place of bow and rifle hunters, stalking the deer and the elk as did the Apache and the Mogollon before them. At night the winter constellations, ruled by that great formation of bright stars known as

Orion, begin to make their appearance. By November many of the birds of summer have departed to winter in Baja and points farther south, and, in some desolate canyon or twilight forest, the bears have climbed sleepily into their warm, bough- and moss-lined dens.

WINTER.   (November through February) The winter is not nearly as severe in the mountains of the Gila Wilderness as in the Rockies, just a few hundred miles to the north. At the lower elevations, temperatures may climb into the low 60s during the day. It is a popular time to cross-country ski on the Crest Trail or the Holt-Apache Trail, or to hike in the dry lower canyons. There are few if any visitors to the Gila at this time of the year and you can have parts of it all to yourself. The hot springs are always a good place on a mild winter day to sit and dream of summers past or summers yet to come. There are days when you can visit such a place, normally quite crowded at other times of the year, and not see a single soul. That is the beauty of winters in the Gila country, when you share the wilderness with only the rabbits and the owls, the deer and the elk, the coyotes and the lions, as if it were your own private sanctuary.

HAZARDS IN THE WILDERNESS

At certain times of the year, and in certain situations, the Gila can be a formidable and even deadly wilderness. The rugged and remote character of the terrain, coupled with the isolated nature of many trails, always presents a challenge to the backcountry traveler, particularly one who is alone or inexperienced. Always inform someone of your route and take maps and a compass together with plenty of water and extra clothes in case the weather changes. The following is a list of the more common hazards in the wilderness and how to avoid them. As a general rule, the most important thing to remember is, when traveling in areas far from other human beings, always err on the side of caution. The list is alphabetical and not ordered according to the respective importance or severity of particular hazards.

BEARS.   Bears are not too much of a problem in the Gila Wilderness, but a few basic common sense rules need to be kept in mind. Never approach an unattended cub. The sow is always nearby. Never leave food unattended around camp. Always cook and then hoist food supplies into a tree some distance from your sleeping area. Never camp in an area where you observe fresh bear droppings, diggings, or tracks. If you surprise a bear in camp or while out hiking in the backcountry, don't run: the bear will interpret this as a sign of fear, which will simply trigger the animal's instinct to attack. If the bear shows signs of advancing, throw down your pack to distract and delay him. Walk calmly to the nearest tree and climb it as high as you can. In the extremely rare case in which you are actually attacked, play dead with your knees tucked against your chest and your hands placed behind your head and neck. The likelihood of a bear attack occurring is probably the same as being attacked by a shark at Coney Island. Actually it is probably far less. No such incidents have occurred in the Gila in recent memory. Rattlesnakes are a greater threat in the Gila.

BEING LOST.   If you find yourself lost, don't panic. The most important thing is to relax and to calm down. Sit down, study your surroundings and maps, and listen for sounds that may give you a clue as to your whereabouts. Look for a familiar peak, saddle, or ridge.

If you find yourself lost, look for a familiar peak, saddle, or ridge. Here above the Granny Mountain Trail, for example, Brushy Mountain is visible to the south. (Photograph by John Murray)

Remember that the sun and moon rise and set from east to west. If you don't have a compass, examine the foilage to determine the north-to-south orientation of vegetation patterns. Remember that north slopes are more heavily forested in the mountains. All major drainages soon lead to civilization. If you must spend an unplanned night in the Gila, there are many natural shelters in the form of caves and openings in the rock as well as cover provided by fallen trees. Always carry emergency gear in your daypack, particularly when you are exploring from your base camp and do not have your horses or your backpack. A daypack should include such items as matches, a candle, lighter fluid, flashlight, compass, poncho, water, food (including at least one meal in addition to energy foods), heavier clothing (a hat, gloves, parka, sweater or jacket), map, fish hooks and line, and a good knife. The most common time for people to become lost or disoriented is in their day hikes from their base camp. If you do not return at the time you have told friends, help will soon arrive. Probably the most important thing in any crisis is to have a sense of humor and a little common sense. The wilderness can either be an old friend or a clever enemy when you are lost. It all depends on you.

DANGEROUS INSECTS.   The most dangerous insect found in the Gila is the scorpion whose sting is quite painful, something like that of a sea urchin spine. The tarantula also inhabits the area and produces a painful bite with its fangs which are located on the abdomen. In both cases, the most important thing is to thoroughly cleanse the affected area to prevent infection, and to seek prompt medical attention. Incidents with either one are uncommon. Those allergic to bees and wasps should carry appropriate medication.

FLASH FLOODS.   Sudden, heavy runoff from snowmelt or seasonal rains from mid-July to mid-September can cause flash floods. Extremely localized or torrential downpours at or near the headwaters of a stream or river can result in extremely dangerous flash floods. The narrow box canyons found in the Gila Wilderness can put hikers or horsemen in a deadly situation at these times. A flood on December 18, 1978 washed out almost all the bride approaches at the confluence of the West and East forks, as well as uprooting trees several feet in diameter. It is not wise to camp in canyon bottoms during the normal flash flood season. Be certain to check with rangers and inquire as to local weather forecasts at that time. This is a hazard to be taken very seriously.

FORDING STREAMS AND RIVERS.   Every year many people drown in the streams and rivers of the West, most often during the spring runoff. Most of these fatalities can be attributed to simple lack of experience or bad judgment. Frequently, the victims are from other parts of the country and are unaware of the danger of mountain water, of its often surprising depth and velocity. Do not attempt to cross any moving water that appears even remotely hazardous. Many crossings are impossible in the spring or after a heavy summer rain. This is particularly true along the Gila River and its three forks upstream. During runoff, rivers are lowest in the early morning. A good precaution before entering the water is to release the waist strap and one shoulder strap of your backpack, so that it can be easily jettisoned if the current sweeps you off your feet. A walking stick is always helpful in maintaining balance and for probing the cobblestone bottom for safe footing. Tennis shoes are helpful for the many river crossings. Always carry waterproof safety matches in a pocket of your trousers or shirt. In the event that you are separated from your pack and left soaking wet deep in the wilderness, you will then have the means to dry and warm yourself.

FOREST FIRE.   The mountains and canyons of the Gila country can become quite dry at times and are very susceptible to fire. Remember a few simple rules. Whenever possible, use a gas stove. If you must have a campfire, dig down to the mineral soil in the immediate vicinity of the fire. Avoid fires on a windy night. Don't waste a lot of firewood on unnecessarily large fires. Never break branches from standing trees. Extinguish all fires before leaving the area. Scatter and bury the ashes and restore the natural appearance of the area. Above all, never smoke on the trail.

GIARDIA LAMBLIA.   Giardia is an intestinal parasite found in animal feces, particularly beaver, which pollutes mountain water and causes serious gastrointestinal symptoms referred to medically as *giardiasis*. Nicknamed "Beaver Fever" in the mountains, it is even more debilitating than *turista*, which often afflicts travelers south of the border. Symptoms include painful intestinal cramps, gas, and severe diarrhea. Dehydration, dizziness, disorientation, and extreme listlessness and fatigue can result. Medical attention should be sought. It is important to keep fluid and salt levels up. To avoid such cases of dysentary, boil or chemically treat all water in the Gila. No water, standing or running, can be considered safe.

HEART FAILURE.   At the first sign of pain, numbness, tingling in the chest, neck, or arms, or extreme dizziness or faint-headedness, immediately suspend all strenuous physical activities, descend to lower elevation where necessary, and seek medical assistance. Even young adults, people in their thirties, have succumbed to heart failure in the wilderness. People whose family trees indicate a history of this problem, or who are overweight, who have a sedentary lifestyle, who

River crossings are generally safe during the summer when the water is low. Author is pictured here on the West Fork in late August. (Photograph by Charles William Murray, Junior)

smoke, or who have a combination of these factors, should be particularly cognizant of this very real danger.

HEAT STRESS DISORDERS.   There are three forms of heat stress disorder, all of which sometimes afflict travelers in the Gila country: heat cramps, heat exhaustion, and heat stroke. Maintaining a high level of physical fitness and awareness as well as properly maintaining fluid levels is the best protection against heat stress. The physically fit person has a well-developed circulatory capacity as well as increased blood volume, both important in regulating internal body temperature. *Heat cramps* are caused by salt lost through sweating. Treatment includes stretching the affected muscle as well as drinking athletic drinks or lightly salted water, lemonade, or juice. *Heat exhaustion*, a more serious condition, results from extreme heat together with water loss through sweating. Symptoms include weakness, unstable gait, fatigue, wet and clammy skin, headache, nausea, and physical collapse. Get the victim to shade or into water and administer lightly salted fluids. *Heat stroke* is the most dangerous heat stress disorder of all. This is a life-threatening situation. Body temperature can soar to levels as high as 105 degrees Fahrenheit. All sweating stops. Brain damage, convulsions, and delirium commences. It is absolutely imperative that the victim be immediately immersed in cold water or soaked in any kind of liquid available and vigorous fanning begun. This should all be done in the shade. Treat the victim for shock. Heat stroke is a medical emergency. Permanent brain damage and death will quickly result if prompt treatment is not given.

HOT SPRINGS.   The geothermal springs in the Gila Wilderness range widely in temperature, from the tepid (80 degrees Fahrenheit) to the pleasantly hot (103 degrees Fahrenheit) to the dangerously hot (140 degrees Fahrenheit). To avoid scalding, always carefully test the water before submerging any large portions of your body. Also, there has been at least one fatal case of a rare form of meningitis carried by an amoeba in a hot spring south of Silver City.

HYPOTHERMIA.   Hypothermia, or exposure, is the rapid, progressive, mental and physical collapse of a person that accompanies the cooling of the inner core of the body. It is caused by a combination of exertion and rain, snow, sleet, or wind and can even occur after crossing or falling into a stream or river. Symptoms include uncontrollable shivering, cold extremities, and a confused and eventually indifferent state of mind. Treatment should never include alcohol, which dilates blood vessels and accelerates heat loss. Treatment should include wrapping the victim in dry warm clothing or a sleeping bag and administering warm fluids. In extreme cases, it might be advisable for another individual to enter the sleeping bag in order to transfer body heat.

HYPOXIA.   Also known as altitude or mountain sickness, hypoxia afflicts some people at elevations above 8,000 feet. It has a variety of symptoms, some as mild as a headache, nausea, a feeling of weakness or indolence, and a poor appetite. More serious symptoms include dizziness, hyperventilation, disorientation, impaired judgment, retinal bleeding, blurred vision, and, in the most severe cases, pulmonary edema. The victim should descend to lower altitude and seek medical assistance.

LIGHTNING.   Severe electrical storms accompanied by rain are common in the summer. Lightning is the chief hazard of these storms. Lightning prefers to strike as a down or an upstroke the highest point or peak, the edge of cliffs, isolated trees or rocks, or the largest object in an open area. Storms rarely develop without giving the traveler ample warning so that proper precautions might be taken. If, however, you are caught in a bad situation, authorities recommend that you crouch down (not lie down) on some kind of dry, insulating material, such as a sleeping bag. Remove all metallic objects as they will cause serious burns if you are electrocuted. Avoid cliff faces as the exploding bolt will radiate out from the rock. Also avoid shallow caves. If a companion is struck by lightning, immediately begin closed heart massage, mouth-to-mouth resuscitation, and if the victim is revived, treat for shock.

PLAGUE.   Bubonic plague, a disease carried by rodents transmitted by fleas, is widespread in the western United States. Plague is firmly entrenched among the wild rodents in this region, and individual cases continue to occur among humans exposed to the disease. Incidents of human mortality are known in Colorado, Utah, and New Mexico. Plague is most often found in rock squirrels, prairie dogs, wood rats, and other species of ground squirrel and chipmunk. Wild rabbits also become involved in the plague cycle. The bacterium *Yersinia pestis* is transmitted to human beings both through flea bite and direct contact with infected animals. Rock squirrels are one of the more significant plague hosts in the area. Their principal flea (*Diamanus montanus*) is an aggressive parasite and will readily bite other animals including domestic cats and dogs as well as people. In man, the incubation period (interval between exposure and appearance of symptoms) is usually two to six days. Symptoms include sudden onset of fever and chills, severe headache, muscle aches, nausea, vomiting, and a general feeling of systemic illness. Extreme pain and swelling in a lymph node draining the infection site is also a suggested symptom. Other forms of the disease include septicemic illness with no bubo (swollen lymph gland) developing, and pneumonic plague in which the lungs are involved. Septicemic and pneumonic plague are the most serious forms of the disease. Treatment with antibiotics is effective during the early stages. If diagnosis and treatment are delayed, life-threatening complications may follow. As soon as these symptoms appear, a physician should be consulted and informed of any recent exposure (particularly if the victim is a tourist living in a state where plague is rare or unknown) for appropriate diagnosis. The following precautions should be taken in the Gila country, and elsewhere: 1) Do not feed, play with, or entice any rodent or rabbit species. 2) Avoid rodent harborage or dwellings. 3) Avoid contact with all sick and dead rodents and rabbits. Look for evidence of animal die-offs and report any such areas to local or state health departments. 4) Use insect repellents. 5) Leave pets at home. 6) If you hunt or trap rabbits or carnivorous wild animals such as coyotes and bobcats that prey on rabbits or rodents, protect your hands and face while skinning or handling these animals. Fresh pelts may be treated with flea powder. 7) Any bite from any animal, wild or domestic, may cause plague. In summary, plague infection can be treated successfully and cured if early diagnosis is made. Early treatment is the key. While plague cannot now be eliminated from our natural environment, human cases of the disease can be prevented through simple, common sense measures.

POISON IVY.   Poison ivy (*Rhus radicans*) is common in the richer soils typically found in the riparian woodlands of the Gila Wilderness Area. The plant grows from April through September and can always be recognized by the distinctive pattern of three leflets per leaf. Margins of the leaflets are often notched or toothed. The plant is often found in ravines and canyons up to 8,000 feet, and in places the ivy climbs vinelike over entire trees and shrubs. It contains a volatile oil which can cause painful swelling and eruptions of the skin. Seek medical attention if the inflammation is widespread. Never burn poison ivy branches in campfires. The smoke has caused blindness in some people.

POISONOUS REPTILES.   Four species of rattlesnake are found in the Gila as well as the deadly coral snake and the less dangerous Gila monster. Avoid sticking your hands or arms or head into crevices or among rocks while climbing in the canyons. Avoid all snakes but do not intentionally kill snakes. There is no faster striking snake in the world than the rattlesnake. If bitten, remain calm. Shock increases the flow of the blood and the effects of the poison. Most bites can be survived. The most important thing is to get the victim to a physician immediately.

QUICKSAND.   Quicksand is found along some streams and rivers in the area. Avoid sandy places that appear wet or muddy. If stuck, remove your pack and use your walking stick, accompanied by swimming motions, to extricate yourself. A companion can use a log or vine to pull you free.

ROCK CLIMBING.   Many vacationers are injured and sometimes even killed each year in the West as a result of unsupervised, ill-advised, or amateur rock climbing. Typically, these people climb up a steep slab surface or rock outcropping and discover they cannot retrace their path back down. Suddenly aware of their dangerous situation, they panic and fall. Serious fractures, contusions, lacerations, bruises, concussions, and even paralysis can result. Talus slides also represent more of a hazard than most people believe. It is best to avoid any rock climbing unless experienced, properly equipped, and sufficiently supervised.

SUNBURN.   The high altitude sun of New Mexico can quickly cause severe burns to exposed skin, far worse than at sea level. Chronic exposure to the sun at this elevation destroys the ability of the body to fight back against cancer cells in the epidermis, resulting in skin cancer. These sunbelt areas of the country have much higher rates of skin cancer than other parts of the country. Colorado has the highest rate in the nation. Skin cancer can be fatal when it spreads to other organs and systems of the body and has sometimes killed people in their twenties or thirties. Any unusual pigmented bump or mole appearing on the skin after a bad sunburn or on the skin of a person who is often exposed to the sun should be immediately examined by a physician.

TRAIL CONDITIONS.   In several places the trails are extremely narrow, pass over a rock surface, and/or have many switchbacks. In some of these areas, such as the gorge on the West Fork upstream from the White Creek confluence, horse travel is impossible. Check with rangers before proceeding on any trail with or without livestock.

All people who use the Gila Wilderness and places like it should take the time to learn standard first aid procedures, such as how to treat a fracture, how to treat shock, how to administer cardiopulmonary resuscitation, how to treat a burn, how to treat a bad wound (including gunshot), and how to treat a drowning victim. Just a little bit of knowledge could go a long way to saving a life if you have it. If you don't, you'll be left standing there helplessly while someone suffers a great deal, or, worse, dies. And you'll have ample time to reflect on that old adage, "The wilderness doesn't care."

A WILDERNESS ETHIC

The chief objective of any wilderness ethic is, of course, minimum impact. Travelers should strive to leave the ecosystem exactly as they found it, an undisturbed natural laboratory where the subtle adaptive and creative forces of nature can work freely and without interference by man. With this in mind, a few simple principles should be remembered.

1) Scrupulously obey all official regulations pertaining to travel in the Gila Wilderness, particularly with respect to camping and campfires. Also observe all fish and game regulations.
2) Avoid shortcuts and endeavor to remain on established trails.
3) Camp on nonvegetated soil when possible to avoid killing fragile plants.
4) Be considerate of others when camping and remain as quiet and out of the way as possible.
5) Don't build any permanent structures, like cairns and campfire rings, or scar trees with a knife or axe.
6) Pack out everything you pack in.
7) Use a gas stove when possible.
8) In areas where it is permitted, keep your campfire small and restore the area to its natural appearance before you leave.
9) Don't use soap in or around lakes or streams.
10) Dispose of wastes in holes 6 inches deep and at least 100 feet from any moving or standing water.
11) Never pick wildflowers or disturb wildlife.
12) Leave your pets at home.
13) When approaching horses on the trail, give them the right-of-way, standing on the downhill side of the trail. Any sudden movement can alarm a horse and cause a serious accident for the rider.
14) If you take horses or mules into the backcountry, remember that forage is scarce in many areas. Avoid grazing your stock or turning them loose at night. Instead, string a pack rope between two trees. Tie the lead ropes to this rope short enough so the animals cannot entangle a leg in them. Complete ration

While traveling in the Gila Wilderness, never scar a tree with a knife or an axe. Treat the back-country with reverence, as you would a church, library, or museum. (Photograph by John Murray)

pellets are an excellent food source for your riding and pack-stock. Rolled grains lack sufficient roughage and whole grains eventually sprout and compete with natural vegetation. Always picket your stock away from campsites and especially away from water sources.

15) Do not dig for pottery or artifacts in historic or prehistoric sites.

16) Put your fire out cold before leaving the area. Never smoke while hiking or riding in the backcountry.

17) Many people are finding that alternative footwear is better than the vibram-soled waffle stompers that were popular in the sixties and seventies. Some of these boots were simply too heavy and uncomfortable and often caused blisters. Light footwear is in addition to being more comfortable far less destructive of trails, particularly in sensitive regions.

CAMERAS IN THE DESERT MOUNTAINS

Whether you travel on foot, by horse, or on skis, you will probably take a camera with you. The scenery throughout the Wilderness is quite spectacular and lends itself to nature photography. Bright colors, deep shadows, long vistas, interesting structures, and unusual textures abound. Basic equipment should include a 35mm camera, at least one roll of 36 exposures for each day on the trail, and lens cleaner. Beyond that most serious photographers would want to carry one or more of the following: a wide angle lens, a 90mm or 135mm telephoto lens (and a tripod if you pack a 200mm lens), and a macrolens for closeups of wildflowers (particularly those with a focal length longer than 50mm).

In the high country there are extremely sharp lighting contrasts. Use a light meter, preferably one that measures spot as well as average readings. Water, snow, sand, and sky will fool your meter. Open the diaphragm two stops more than the meter indicates in order to compensate for glare. At higher elevations there is so much light coming from the sky that your meter will be confused. For more realistic readings, aim the meter more toward the ground than you normally would. If your camera has a lens meter, it lacks the accuracy of a separate meter. With the attached meter, you are more likely of getting the photo you want if you bracket the shot with several exposures. A medium-speed color film should handle most situations you're likely to encounter. It gives you more flexibility in dark forests and handles all lighting with more color warmth than high-speed film. Use a medium yellow filter if you're shooting black and white.

Remember that even with the greatest nature photographers only a small percentage of the pictures they take are worthy of being enlarged and put under glass. Wild animals are notoriously difficult to photograph because of their quick, unpredictable movements. A long distance shot is sometimes best put into perspective with an interesting flower or rock framed in the foreground. And finally, the simple addition of a person into a picture can often make it the most memorable of all, either a companion with you on the trail or some new-found friend in the wilderness.

River Rafting on the Gila

The section of the Gila River between the Highway 15 bridge and the Turkey Creek confluence above the town of Cliff is a popular area in the early spring with river rafters. Some of the most rugged and spectacular country in the Southwest can be seen on a float trip between these two points. Farther downstream and outside the Gila Wilderness, the Gila River between Cliff and Redrock in the vicinity of the Big Burro Mountains is also popular with whitewater enthusiasts. That portion of the river is not recommended for beginners as it contains Class IV rapids which flow through narrow, rocky canyons that are extremely hazardous during periods of high water.

The time to float the Gila must be chosen with care since the water levels fluctuate dramatically, even in the spring. The most reliable water flow normally occurs during the runoff from mid–March through mid-April. The water usually peaks in the last week of March or in the first week of April, but some years the flow has been down to 400 cubic feet per second by the end of March. As a general rule, 750 cubic feet per second is about the minimum required to run the river, but many with smaller craft float it at far less. With flow rates below 750 cubic feet per second, the river averages 2 to 4 feet in depth. With the river at 200 cubic feet per second or more, it is floatable in small boats that draft less than 3 or 4 inches. At such levels, the larger boats are definitely not recommended.

The total distance of the journey is just over 32 miles. Most groups float it in around five days. The takeout point can be reached via State Road 293 and Forest Road 155 (see Turkey Creek Trail description). Forest Road 155, which is steep and rough and can become muddy and slick when wet, comes to a dead end just below the confluence of Turkey Creek and the Gila River. An alternative to this route is to float downriver an additional nine miles to the townsite of Gila.

The river can be run in canoes, kayaks, and tubes. The preferred mode of travel for most is by specialized whitewater crafts. A life vest and headgear should be worn. Spare paddles, waterproof bags, plenty of repair materials, and extra food provisions should be carried because of the extreme remoteness of the area. Sapillo Creek (see Spring

Canyon Trail description), located approximately 15 miles downstream from the Highway 15 bridge, is the only foot exit once the trip is begun. The walk out from this juncture is 6.5 miles.

The river is mainly Class I, but there are series of Class II and Class III rapids. The stream is rocky in places but the primary hazard is sharp bends around which are fallen trees and an occasional barbed wire fence. These logjams and stock guards may require a portage. It is always a good idea to inspect rapids before an attempt is made to run them. A favorite place of river rafters downstream is the Turkey Creek Hot Spring (see Turkey Creek Trail description). Always be alert for hypothermia in the cold spring waters.

Weather is variable at this time of year—there may be anything from rain to snowfall—but normally the days are warm and sunny (75 degrees Fahrenheit) and the nights cool and clear (35 degrees Fahrenheit). Because of the short and sometimes unpredictable river-running season on the Gila, generally not very many boaters will be encountered. It is advisable to leave an itinerary of your trip with a friend or relative prior to departure. Never travel alone down the river. When camping on the river, scrupulously obey all written and unwritten regulations pertaining to backcountry travel. Leave only footprints, take only pictures.

Hunting and Fishing

Game animals commonly hunted in the Gila Wilderness include mule deer, white-tailed deer, elk, antelope, cougar, bear, doves, quail, and turkey. Information on hunting is available from the New Mexico Department of Game and Fish, Main Office, State Capitol, Santa Fe, New Mexico, 87501; (505) 827-2143. Some permits and licenses must be applied for before the season.

Fishing is also a popular activity in the Gila Wilderness. Licenses and information with specific requirements and restrictions are available from a variety of local vendors or from the Department of Game and Fish. Many of the lakes outside the Wilderness are stocked with rainbow trout, including the following: Lake Roberts, Quemado Lake, Snow Lake, Bear Canyon Reservoir, Bill Evans Lake, and Wall lake. Creeks offering trout include the following: Gilita, Iron, Little, Mogollon, Negrito, Turkey, White, Whitewater, and Willow. The three forks of the Gila River above the bridge on New Mexico 15 also have trout. Below this bridge are trout, bass, and catfish. Certain streams in the Wilderness are closed to fishing in order to protect the rare native fish, the Gila trout (check with rangers if you have any questions on this). Both the Tularosa River and the San Francisco River contain trout in the upper regions with catfish downstream.

The Gila Cliff Dwellings National Monument

The Gila Cliff Dwellings National Monument, managed by the Forest Service personnel at the Gila Wilderness Ranger Station, is located in the most commonly used access point to the Gila Wilderness. It is one of the finest examples of ancient architecture in the region and should be included in the itinerary of anyone visiting the area. A ranger is normally stationed in the dwellings to answer questions. The site is open from 8:00 A.M. to 5:00 P.M. every day of the year except December 25 and January 1. It is about an hour and a half drive north of Silver City on New Mexico 15. There is no public transportation to the monument. Camping and picnic areas are available nearby. Groceries and gas can be obtained at the store in Gila Hot Springs, a few miles down the road.

Cliff Dweller Canyon, in which the ruins are located, is a deep canyon with a narrow mouth, carrying a permanent stream that flows northeast into the nearby West Fork. The walls of the canyon, composed of volcanic tuff, are from 100 to 300 feet high. Numerous rock caves and natural shelters abound in the rock. After leaving the bottom of the canyon about 300 yards above the bridge, the trail climbs to the right at which point the cliff dwellings become visible. The largest and most impressive structures are found in the "Triple Cave," which has three distinct openings separated by two large natural pillars. The cave is as long as a football field, runs up to 30 feet high, and extends 50 feet back into the rock. The builders constructed their plazas, apartments, circular kiva, and storage bins from materials found in the area. The masonry is always joined directly to the rock. Wooden support timbers can still be seen. Some of the original rafters give evidence of having deen destroyed by fire, which may or may not be related to the sudden abandonment of the site in prehistoric times. Before excavation by scientists, the caves contained considerable pottery, hundreds of corn cobs, fragments of obsidian, flint, broken arrow points, yucca fibre string, a mummy, and lower and upper milling stones (metate and mano).

Although the earliest part of the monument, a pithouse, was made sometime between A.D. 100 and 400, most of the major construction occurred at a later time. The pithouse type of architecture persisted until about A.D. 1000. Square houses built above ground then became the favored form of house building. Additionally, a new form of white pottery with black designs appeared at about the same time. Authorities refer to this skillfully painted pottery as "Classic Mimbres." The cliff dwellings were probably constructed after A.D. 1000.

There are about 40 rooms built into the major southeast-facing cave. It is thought that no more than 10 to 15 families occupied this particular site at any one time. Roof timbers from the monument date up into the 1280s. The residents farmed on the mesa tops and along the river, raising squash, beans, corn, and, most likely, amaranth and tobacco. This diet was supplemented with wild animals, wild berries, and naturally occurring nuts. In many ways, the diet of the Mogollon was probably more healthy than that of many Americans today.

Sometime in the last years of the thirteenth century, in an event still little understood, this promising culture left the area. It is not known why this occurred, although there is no shortage of theories. In the years that followed members of the last wave of emigrants from Asia, the Athapascans, began to arrive in the area. They never occupied the cliff dwellings and adopted a hunting/gathering lifestyle. These people eventually became what we know today as the Apache and Navajo.

A Note on Archaeological Sites

The Gila Wilderness and its environs contain many archaeological sites, some dating back to the period of Christ, others as recent as the years around World War I. All of these prehistoric and historic sites, including the Gila Cliff Dwellings National Monument, are managed by the Forest Service in accordance with federal and state laws protecting artifacts and sites on public lands. Since 1979 increased fines and penalties, including imprisonment, have had to be imposed on criminal vandalization and theft in these cultural locations. It is extremely important that you do not disturb these sites. If you make a discovery in the backcountry, which is possible, report it to the forest rangers. Above all, do not disturb it. Professional archaeologists can then examine these remains and, using the latest methods of recovery, dating, and analysis, interpret them with greater accuracy than the amateur. This adds to our knowledge of the past, including why the Mogollon civilization went into a state of decline, and can perhaps better assist our leaders in coping with the same problems as they are found today in the desert Southwest.

An arrowhead, a stone tool, a piece of pottery, a bit of timber embedded in a ruin, are, to the uninformed, mere curiosities, or, to the unscrupulous, simply objects to be used for personal gain. However small and seemingly unimportant, these objects provide important links with the past. A single arrowhead, bit of pottery, military button, or coin may be the only clue left to date and to determine the significance of a cultural site. Once it has been removed from its original location, it is as though an entire page has been torn from the only book on the history of the place and thrown into the wind. Found by a properly trained scientist, though, and studied by such methods as X-ray flourescence spectrometry and obsidian hydration analysis, a single object can provide a wealth of information on the people who left it there. If you do in fact have further interest along these lines, there are amateur archaeological societies in New Mexico and elsewhere that participate in field projects organized by colleges, universities, and the government. A summer on such a dig, or even a week, can be a fascinating and rewarding experience.

PART 4.

WILDERNESS TRAILS

I rode up the Gila River to Turkey Creek, then up Turkey to Little Creek, where I went out on the high prairie to look for fires. Then I rode on through McKenna Park. . . . I traveled on up the West Fork of the Gila to White Creek where I knew I would find good grass. There by the old Jenks Cabin I made camp. That was my headquarters camp year after year, and finally the White Creek Ranger Station was built there.

> —Henry Woodrow, the first forest guard in the Gila
> Wilderness and later district ranger for over thirty years
> (from his *History of McKenna Park District*)

TRAILS OF THE GLENWOOD RANGER DISTRICT

I would rather understand one cause than be King of Persia.
                    —Democritus of Abdera (Fifth Century B.C.)

CREST TRAIL (U.S.F.S. #182)

Trailhead elevation (Sandy Point): 9,132 feet
Trail ending (Mogollon Baldy Lookout): 10,770 feet
Total vertical ascent: 1,638 feet
Length: 12.00 miles (19.20 kilometers)
Recommended season: April through November (Snows
    sometimes close the trail early or linger into the spring).
Use: Moderate
Difficulty: Difficult
U.S.G.S. maps: Grouse Mountain, Mogollon Baldy Peak

Access: Proceed north of Silver City on U.S. 180 past,
consecutively, Cliff (just past the bridge over the main fork of
the Gila River), Buckthorn, Leopold Vista Historical
Monument (well worth the stop), Soldier Hill (just before
Dry Creek, the site of one of the last battles between
Geronimo and the U.S. Army), Pleasanton, and Glenwood
(District Ranger Station is located here). Three miles north of
Glenwood, turn right on New Mexico 78 (if you reach Alma a
mile down the road, you've gone too far). At mile 8.5 is
Mogollon, a historic mining town. Continue past Mogollon
east another 8.0 miles to Sandy Point, just past Whitetail
Canyon, where there is a turnoff on the north side of the road.
The trailhead is well marked on the south side of the road.
The road is unpaved for part of the way past Mogollon, but
presents no problem for two-wheel drive vehicles. The road is
hazardous for trailers longer than 16 feet.

The Crest Trail, one of the more popular trails in the Glenwood
District, offers backcountry visitors an excellent route into the high
Mogollon country. En route to the trailhead is the fascinating relic
town of Mogollon along Silver Creek Canyon, site of a once-thriving
gold and silver mine. Today only a dozen or so people live in the ghost
town year-round, but once thousands made their residence here.

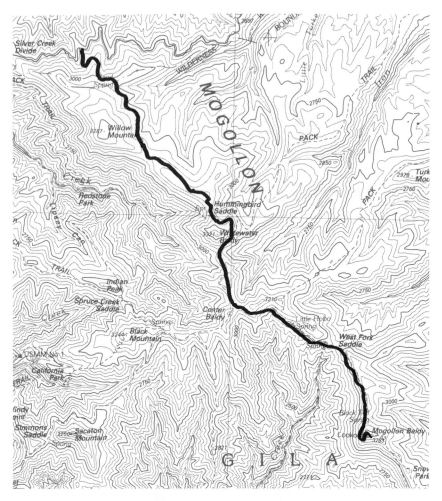

CREST TRAIL   Contour interval 50 meters

From the early 1880s until the early 1940s, more than 19 million dollars in precious metals were extracted from the mines. The Last Chance Shaft, over 1,200 feet deep, contacted a silver vein ranging from 6 to 30 feet wide. The Mogollon Museum makes an interesting stop along the way. Today most people come looking for a different sort of wealth, that of a vast and beautiful wilderness area. The

Whitewater Baldy, at 10,895 feet the highest point in the Gila Wilderness, as seen from Hummingbird Saddle. (Photograph by John Murray)

mountains are now much as they were in 1870, when Sergeant James Cooney, on patrol against the Apaches in Silver Creek Canyon, first discovered silver.

The trail quickly climbs from the road at Sandy Point and ascends a 10,000-foot ridge, which it follows most of the way to Mogollon Baldy Peak, passing Whitewater Baldy (10,895 feet—highest point in the Wilderness) and Center Baldy (10,535 feet) along the way. The Crest Trail really offers the grand tour of the Mogollons, including dense spruce-fir stands, waist-deep fern glades, columbine-filled aspen groves, darting hummingbirds, and elusive herds of elk. One of the most breath-taking experiences in the entire Gila Wilderness is breaking out at Hummingbird Saddle (10,400 feet) and gazing up at Whitewater Baldy, which rises majestically from the surrounding mantle of spruce-fir and aspen forests. It was here the Apache came in the summer to hunt the mule deer and the elk which were so important to their way of life, providing clothing, food. tools, and weapons. In the wintertime, when the Crest Trail is snowbound, it offers some of the better cross-country skiing in the Southwest.

One of the significant differences between these mountains and the mountains of Colorado and Wyoming is the absence of water. Along the ridgelines of the Mogollons there is no running water, and hikers must remain conscious of where reliable springs are located as they travel through the backcountry and eventually decide on a suitable place to camp for the night. Year-round water is available at the following springs (mileages given are from Sandy Point): Bead Spring (1.50 miles), Hummingbird Spring (4.75 miles), Hobo Spring (8.50 miles), Little Hobo Spring (10.00 miles), and Blacktail Spring (11.25 miles). All water needs to be purified before drinking.

Important spur trails located along the Crest Trail are as follows, with mileages from Sandy Point: Willow Creek Trail No. 138 at Bead Springs (1.50 miles), Whitewater Canyon Trail No. 207 at Hummingbird Saddle (4.75 miles), Iron Creek Lake Trail No. 172 at Whitewater Baldy (6.25 miles), Big Dry–Holt-Apache Trail No. 181 south of Center Baldy (7.25 miles), Turkeyfeather Pass Trail No. 102 (8.35 miles), West Fork of Mogollon Creek at West Fork Saddle (10.50 miles), and White Creek Trail No. 152 at Mogollon Baldy (12.00 miles).

Although there is no formal trail, Whitewater Baldy can be ascended from the obvious ridgeline due south of Hummingbird Saddle. The roundtrip takes about an hour, and the view from the far side over the headwaters of Whitewater Creek, is superb. The forest here, like that throughout the Mogollons, is filled with the chattering of sentrylike squirrels. The tracks of coyotes, lions, bears, deer, and elk can sometimes be found. Center Baldy is just a little southwest of the trail, and the trail passes over the top of Mogollon Baldy. Snow Park, about a mile past Mogollon Baldy, is also worth the side trip.

WHITEWATER TRAIL (U.S.F.S. #207)

Trailhead elevation (Whitewater Picnic Ground, Catwalk
    National Recreation Trail): 5,100 feet
Trail ending (Hummingbird Saddle): 10,400 feet
Total vertical ascent: 5,300 feet
Length: 16.75 miles (26.80 kilometers)
Recommended season: April through November (Snows
    sometimes close the upper trail early or linger in those
    regions into the spring).
Use: Moderate to heavy
Difficulty: Difficult
U.S.G.S. maps: Holt Mountain, Grouse Mountain

Access: Drive north of Silver City on U.S. 180 past,
consecutively, Cliff, Buckhorn, Leopold Vista Historical
Monument, Soldier Hill, and Pleasanton to the town of
Glenwood. After crossing Whitewater Creek on the north end
of town, turn right or east on State Road 95. Proceed
approximately five miles to the Whitewater picnic ground.
The trailhead is located at the far end of the picnic ground and
initially runs north of Whitewater Creek.

A popular trail for fishermen, the Whitewater Trail follows Whitewater Creek from the lower canyon, close to its confluence with the
historic San Francisco River, over 16 miles to the main 10,000-foot
ridge of the Mogollon Mountains. Travelers should note that the total
vertical ascent along this distance is over one mile, the greatest climb
in all of the Gila Wilderness. Water is more readily available on this
trail than on some of the others in the Mogollon Mountains, such as
the Crest Trail, because the trail parallels the stream for almost the
entire distance. Good year-round water is available throughout the
trip, except for a two-mile stretch east of the old powerhouse site
where the trail climbs above the creek on the south-facing slope and at
the point where the trail leaves the creek above Redstone Park and

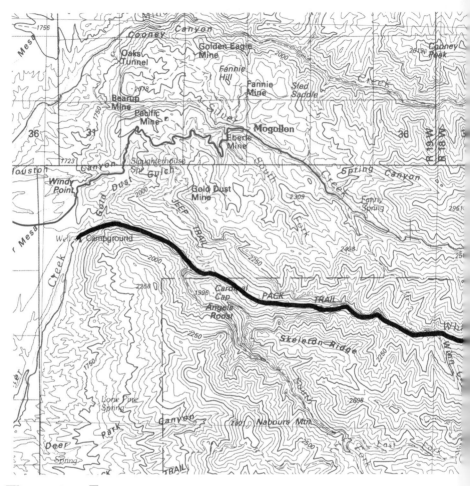

WHITEWATER TRAIL

climbs three miles to Hummingbird Saddle. There is a permanent spring at Hummingbird Saddle, surrounded in the summer months by a profusion of beautiful wildflowers, such as bluebells and red columbine; and, as the name suggests, the site is often visited by hummingbirds as well. Most common is the broad-tailed hummingbird (*Selasphorus platycercus*). Hummingbirds are one of the few birds that feed on nectar, an energy-rich food source necessary for

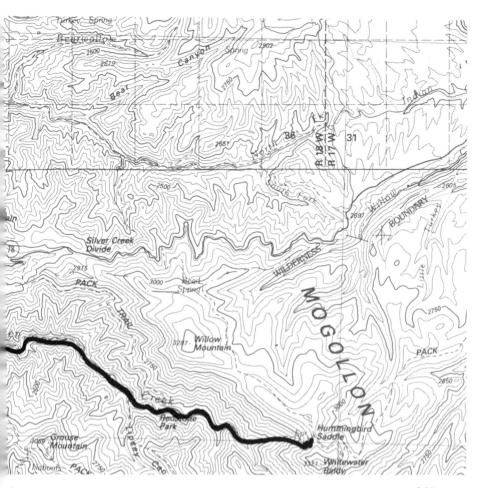

Contour interval 50 meters

their high metabolism. They supplement that diet with insects. Hummingbirds are the chief pollinator for some flowers, particularly red flowers for which they have a preference.

The Whitewater Trail begins at a point of some historic interest in the region. The same boom that created Mogollon spilled over into the surrounding hills and valleys of the area. Prospectors eventually found gold and silver higher up on Whitewater Creek. The narrow

The famous catwalk on the lower White Water Trail. (Photograph by John Murray)

canyon made mining and ore extraction difficult. Water was available year-round higher up in the canyon, but often dried up where the town was located. In 1893 John Graham built a mill to process crude ore midway between the town and the canyon mines. Water was supplied both to the mill and to the town by installing a four-inch metal pipe that clung to the side of the canyon. This was considered quite an engineering feat for the time. Brace holes were drilled into solid rock walls and wooden and iron support bars set in them. The line was protected from freezing by sawdust encased in wood. Four years later a large 18-inch pipe was installed to carry even more water. Repairmen who had to walk the pipeline dubbed it, appropriately, "The Catwalk." The town of Graham only lasted some ten years, and the Graham Mill was never a great success. Today remnants of the mill can still be seen clinging to the north side of the canyon wall at the entrance to the Catwalk. The present metal Catwalk through the deep and narrow gorge of Whitewater Creek was built by the Forest Service in 1961 and is one of the chief recreational attractions of this part of the Gila country. The Catwalk Trail has recently been reconstructed due to the disastrous floods of 1983 and 1984.

Important spur trails located along the Whitewater Trail are as follows, with distances from the Whitewater Picnic Ground: Gold Dust Trail No. 41 (1.00 miles), South Fork Trail No. 212 (2.25 miles), Deloche Trail No. 179 (6.25 miles), Redstone Trail No. 206 (10.50 miles from Catwalk), Redstone Trail No. 206 (North Fork to N.M. #78, 10.75 miles), and the Crest Trail (16.75 miles) on Hummingbird Saddle.

The backcountry traveler can expect to see quite a few day hikers in the vicinity of the Catwalk, but the crowds generally thin out by Winn Canyon (Deloche Trail No. 179). Some of the better fishing in the Wilderness can sometimes be found on Whitewater Creek. The trail is open year-round from the Catwalk to Redstone Park. It may be snowbound from Redstone Park to Hummingbird Saddle between December and April.

The trail offers excellent opportunities for the amateur naturalist to observe the subtle blending of the major life zones of the Gila Wilderness, from the riparian deciduous forest and semidesert brush of the lower creek through the piñon-juniper communities to the evergreen forests and aspen groves of the high country. The Whitewater Trail is an excellent trail for amateur ornithologists as well. Water ouzel (*Cinclus mexicanus*) and canyon wren (*Catherpes mexicanus*) are commonly found along the Catwalk. Down lower, in the piñon-juniper woodlands, observant birdwatchers can spot the ash-throated flycatcher (*Myiarchus cinerascens*) pursuing large flying insects, or the black-throated gray warbler (*Dendroica nigrescens*), whose drab coloring is well adapted to the bluish gray-green of the junipers. In the mixed deciduous woodland along the stream, the solitary vireo (*Vireo solitarius*) is sometimes spotted though more often heard singing its cheerful song: "Chuwee, Cheereo, Bzurrp, Chuweer," The song of most vireos consists of a variety of staccato notes, the basic theme being, "Vi-rio, Vi-reii, Vi-reyo" (with the accent on the second syllable). The authorities who first named the genus in 1807 heard in the bird's song the Latin word *vireo*, meaning "I am green." In the highest coniferous forests the Townsend's solitaire (*Myadestes townsendi*) is often found. Like most thrushes, it forages on the ground for berries and insects and builds its nest on the ground as well, in holes, among exposed roots, and in talus slides. Also, like other thrushes, it is a fine singer, uttering a loud, melodious song with fluty rising and falling phrases.

HOLT-APACHE TRAIL (U.S.F.S. #181)

Trailhead elevation (Sheridan Corrals): 6,500 feet
Trail ending (Crest Trail just east of Center Baldy): 10,320 feet
Total vertical ascent: 3,820 feet
Length: 18.50 miles (29.60 kilometers)
Recommended season: April through November (Snows
  sometimes close the trail early or linger into the spring).
Use: Moderate
Difficulty: Difficult
U.S.G.S. maps: Holt Mountain, Grouse Mountain, Mogollon
  Baldy Peak

Access: Drive north of Silver City on U.S. 180 past,
consecutively, Cliff, Buckthorn, Leopold Vista Historical
Monument, and Soldier Hill. Turn right or east on Forest
Service Route 146, about two miles north of Soldier Hill. (If
you reach Plesanton, you have gone about four miles too far).
Drive four miles northeast on F.S. 146 to the corrals (Sheridan
Corrals) at the end of the road. Trailhead 661 to the Holt-
Apache Trail is located 0.25 miles east of the corrals.

The Holt-Apache Trail, like the Whitewater Trail, leads from the
lower extremes of the Gila Wilderness along the western canyons to
the upper extremes along the crest of the Mogollon Mountains.
Unlike the Whitewater Trail, however, it does not follow one water-
shed in that process, but climbs out of Sheridan Gulch fairly early and
makes its ascent to the high country by way of Holt Mountain (9,750
feet), Grouse Mountain (10,135 feet), Indian Peak (10,115 feet), and
Black Mountain (10,643 feet). These four mountains are formed like a
series of bumps on a long ridge-line complex extending west from
Center Baldy (10,535 feet). Additionally, the Holt-Apache Trail does
not have the great vertical ascent of the Whitewater Trail, making it
more attractive to the foot traveler. Total distance of the two trails is

A stretch of high timber on the Holt–Apache trail. (Photograph by John Murray)

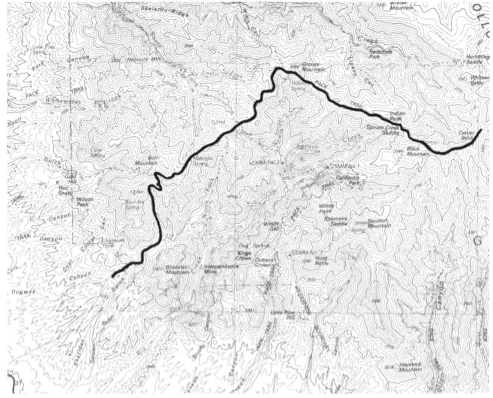

HOLT–APACHE TRAIL   Contour interval 50 meters

approximately the same. Both are very popular trails in this part of
the Gila Wilderness.

As might be expected for a trail that does not follow a stream, water
is scarce for most of the way along the Holt-Apache Trail. In the early
spring and periodically during the late summer, Sheridan Gulch runs
good water. Five miles from the trailhead, good water can be found at
Holt Spring, located just off the trail on the southwest flank of Holt
Mountain. Nabours Spring offers another reliable source 10.5 miles
from the trailhead. Nabours Spring is located 0.25 miles off the main
trail on U.S.F.S. Trail #129, at the headwaters of Spider Creek on the
southwest flank of Grouse Mountain. A third good source is the

Black Mountain Spring (formerly the Stove Pipe Springs), located 14.5 miles from the trailhead just east of the Spruce Creek Saddle on the northeast flank of Black Mountain. Other springs found along the trail, which will probably need purifying, are as follows: Midnite Springs (located 7.0 miles from the trailhead approximately 300 yards from the trail down in the North Fork of Dry Creek), Rock Springs (located 9.0 miles from the trailhead just past the junction with U.S.F.A. Trail #212 and Camp Creek Saddle), Apache Springs (located 15.0 miles from the trailhead on U.S.F.S. Trail #180 east of Black Mountain and about 25 yards from the trail).

Important spur trails along the Holt–Apache Trail are as follows, with distances from the Sheridan Corrals: Piney Basin Trail No. 225 (2.00 miles), Pleasanton Trail No. 217 at Holt Springs (5.00 miles), South Fork Whitewater Trail No. 212 (8.50 miles), Camp Creek Trail No. 218 (8.50 miles), East Fork Whitewater Trail No. 213 (10.00 miles), Deloche Trail No. 179 (10.25 miles), Spider Creek Trail No. 219 (10.50 miles), Redstone Trail No. 206 (13.50 miles), Golden Link Trail No. 218 (15.00 miles), and Sacaton Trail No. 180 (15.25 miles).

The Holt–Apache Trail is often snowbound between December and April. In years of good snowfall, it offers excellent ski touring from Holt Mountain to Sandy Point (by way of the Crest Trail). The view from Grouse Mountain, in particular, is outstanding and provides a commanding overlook from which to survey the Mogollon country, and to look even farther. "The good of going into the mountains," Emerson wrote, "is that life is reconsidered."

SOUTH FORK WHITEWATER TRAIL (U.S.F.S. #212)

Trailhead elevation (old powerhouse site): 6,700 feet
Trail ending (Camp Creek Saddle): 8,480 feet
Total vertical ascent: 1,780 feet
Length: 7.00 miles (11.20 kilometers
Recommended season: April through November (Snows
    sometimes close the trail early and or linger into the spring.
Use: Moderate
Difficulty: Difficult
U.S.G.S. maps: Holt Mountain, Grouse Mountain

Access: Drive west of Silver City on U.S. 180 past,
consecutively, Cliff, Buckthorn, Leopold Vista Historical
Monument, Soldier Hill, and Pleasanton to the town of
Glenwood. After crossing Whitewater Creek on the north end
of town, turn right or east on New Mexico State Highway
#174. Proceed approximately five miles to the Whitewater
Picnic Ground. The South Fork trailhead is located 2.25 miles
from the Catwalk on the Whitewater Trail (U.S.F.S. #207).

The South Fork Trail provides an alternative route into the high
country from the vicinity of the Whitewater Picnic Ground and
Catwalk National Recreation Trail. The trail covers a distance of
seven miles from the powerhouse site and the Camp Creek Saddle,
midway between Holt Mountain (9,750 feet) and Grouse Mountain
(10,135 feet). Good camping sites can be found in this area. The trail
follows the South Fork of Whitewater Creek all the way, with some
very good fishing in places. The narrow rocky gorges offer exceptional scenic beauty and photographic opportunities but should be
watched for potential flash flood hazards. At times seasonal flooding
can make the many creek crossings hazardous. The trail is open year-
round, except in years of very heavy snowfall. Like the Whitewater
Trail, water can be found in the creek for most of its length.
    Important spur trails along the South Fork Trail are as follows,

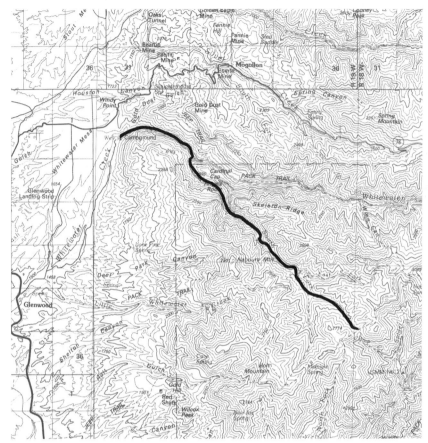

SOUTH FORK WHITEWATER TRAIL   Contour interval 50 meters

with distances from the powerhouse site: East Fork Trail No. 213 at Tennessee Meadows (4.75 miles), Glenwood Trail No. 214 (5.00 miles), and Holt–Apache Trail No. 181 (7.00 miles). The Camp Creek Saddle is a good place from which to launch further explorations into the Mogollon Mountains along the Holt–Apache Trail.

A grove of Arizona sycamores on Whitewater Creek. (Photograph by John Murray)

Trails of the Mimbres Ranger District

Seekers after gold dig up much earth and find little.
                    —Heraclitus of Ephesus (Sixth Century B.C.)

Tom Moore Trail (U.S.F.S. #708)

Trailhead elevation (from the North Star Road at Trailhead 632): 7,600 feet
Trail ending (East Fork of the Gila River): 5,600 feet
Total vertical ascent: 2,000 feet
Length: 15.00 miles (24.00 kilometers)
Recommended season: April through November
Use: Moderate
Difficulty: Moderate
U.S.G.S. maps: Middle Mesa, Gila Hot Springs

Access: Drive north from Silver City on New Mexico 15 towards Pinos Altos. At mile 26.2 is the junction with New Mexico 35 to Lake Roberts and San Lorenzo. Bear left to reach the western end of the trail, which is found at mile 39.4, just before the bridge over the Gila River at the confluence of East and West forks. Take the road on the right at this point, which leads to Lyons Lodge. Trailheads for both #708 and #709 are at the end of the road. At the junction with New Mexico 35 mentioned previously, bear right to reach access to the eastern end of the trail. Continue past Lake Roberts and turn left, or north, on New Mexico 61 at mile 12.6 past the junction. (Warning—do not attempt the Outer Loop Drive, via Beaverhead, without plenty of gas. There are no gas stations between Mimbres and Glenwood, a six-to eight-hour drive, almost all on gravel road). Proceed north on New Mexico 61, also known as the North Star Route, past North Star Mesa, Rocky Canyon Campground, Meason Park, Lower Black Canyon Campground, and Upper Black Canyon Campground approximately 25 miles to the trailhead marked 632 on the left, or west, side of the road.

The Tom Moore Trail, which descends Tom Moore Canyon, crosses Tom Moore Mesa, and then descends the East Fork of the Gila River

The Black Range is visible in the distance from this high point on Tom Moore Mesa. (Photograph by John Murray)

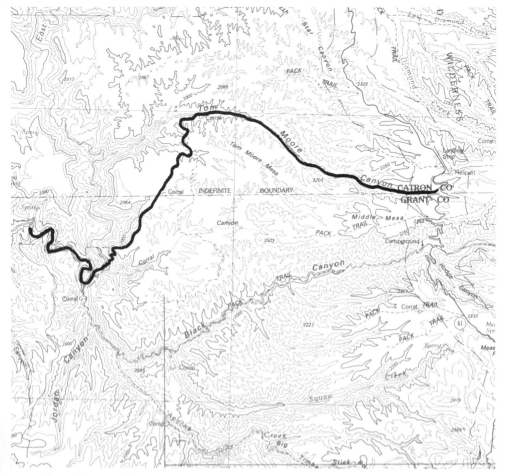

TOM MOORE TRAIL   Contour interval 50 meters

to the Lyons Lodge, is one of the major trails crossing that portion of
the Gila Wilderness that was formerly known as the Gila Primitive
Area, between the North Star Road and New Mexico 15. It covers a
distance of about 15 miles and is for the most part an easy trail,
following an old roadbed to the private land in Tom Moore Canyon.
At this point the trail turns south and passes through some grassy hills

before dropping rapidly into the canyon of the East Fork. The last two miles cross the river in several places which can be very dangerous when the river is at high water. Check with the ranger station before using this part of the trail, particularly in the late spring during the runoff. It may also be too high to cross in the summer after periods of heavy rain upstream.

MIDDLE MESA TRAIL (U.S.F.S. #716)

Trailhead elevation (from the North Star Road at Trailhead 633): 7,600 feet
Trail ending (at junction with U.S.F.S. #708): 6,400 feet
Total vertical ascent: 1,200 feet
Length: 7.75 miles (12.40 kilometers)
Recommended season: April through November
Use: Moderate
Difficulty: Moderate
U.S.G.S. maps: Middle Mesa

Access: Drive north from Silver City on New Mexico 15 towards Pinos Altos. At mile 26.2 is the junction with New Mexico 35 to Lake Roberts and San Lorenzo. Bear right and continue past Lake Roberts 12.6 miles, until the junction with New Mexico 61 is reached. Bear left or north and continue past North Star Mesa, Rocky Canyon Campground, Lower Black Canyon Campground, and Upper Black Canyon Campground to Trailhead 633. The turnoff to the trail from the North Star Road is located in a sharp curve of the road north of Black Canyon. Due to the sloping nature of the curve in the road, it is dangerous to execute a turn at this junction. It is safer to park about 0.25 miles up the road in a small clearing.

The Middle Mesa Trail, which connects with the Tom Moore Trail on the other end, is often used by hikers to make a loop through the heart of what was formerly the Gila Primitive Area. The trail follows the relatively flat, grassy, almost prairielike Middle Mesa in a westerly direction for about 5.0 miles before dropping into Corral Canyon and bearing right, or north, another 2.75 miles to its junction with Tom Moore Trail (U.S.F.S. #708) in the low grassy hillcountry. Like most of the trails in this part of the Wilderness (between New Mexico 15 and New Mexico 61), opportunities abound to view wildlife species

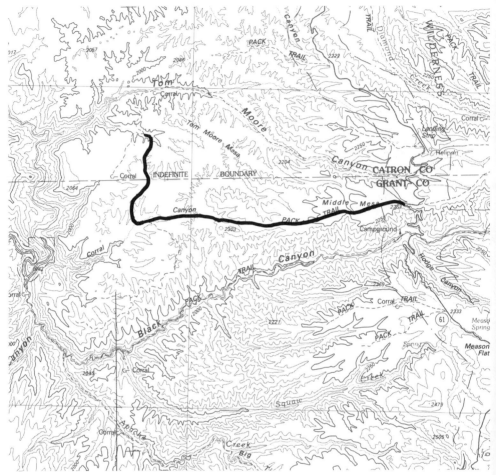

MIDDLE MESA TRAIL   Contour interval 50 meters

such as mule deer, antelope, a variety of squirrels, rabbits, and many birds from meadowlarks to piñon jays to the red-tailed hawks that prey on the prairie dogs. Another species common in the vicinity of the prairie dog communities is the bull snake, which sometimes grows to lengths exceeding six feet. The western diamondback rattlesnake, also inhabiting these areas, is often consumed by the bull snake. This trail is particularly beautiful in the early spring after the snows have melted and the wildflowers have blossomed.

CAVES TRAIL (U.S.F.S. #803)

Trailhead elevation (Rocky Canyon Campground): 7,400 feet
Trail ending (caves area): 7,100 feet
Total vertical ascent: 300 feet
Length: 0.75 miles (1.20 kilometers)
Recommended season: March through November
Use: Heavy
Difficulty: Easy
U.S.G.S. maps: North Star Mesa

Access: Drive north from Silver City on New Mexico 15 towards Pinos Altos. At mile 26.2 is the junction with New Mexico 35 to Lake Roberts and San Lorenzo. Bear right and continue past Lake Roberts 12.6 miles, until the junction with New Mexico 61 is reached. Bear left or north and continue past North Star Mesa to Rocky Canyon Campground, about 15 miles from the junction. The trailhead is found on the west side of the campground (same as Brannon Park Trail #700 for the first 0.25 miles).

Probably the shortest trail in the Gila Wilderness, this 0.75-mile trail follows Rocky Canyon down from the campground to an interesting area of steep cliffs, rock outcroppings, deep gorges, and natural caves. Caution should be exercised if the trail is left, as there are numerous steep dropoffs and slippery spots along the rocks. Children should be closely supervised by parents. Opportunities for interesting photographs abound.

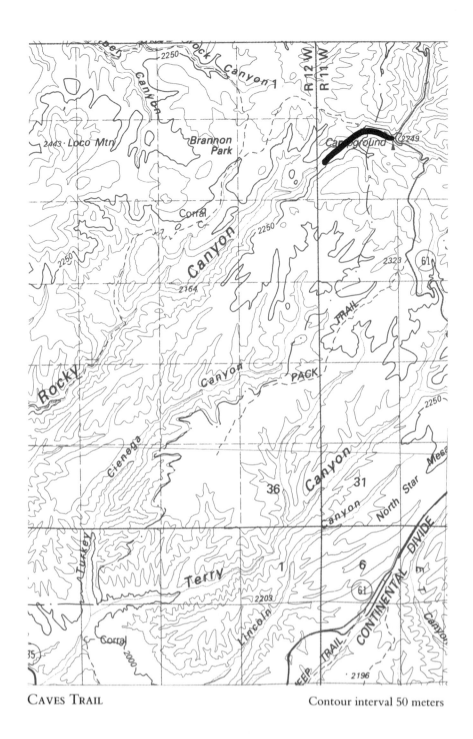

CAVES TRAIL

Contour interval 50 meters

BLACK CANYON TRAIL (U.S.F.S. #94)

Trailhead elevation (Lower Black Canyon Campground):
  7,100 feet
Trail ending (Lower Black Canyon): 6,300 feet
Total vertical ascent: 800 feet
Length: 3.00 miles (4.80 kilometers)
Recommended season: April through November
Use: Moderate
Difficulty: Easy
U.S.G.S. maps: Middle Mesa

Access: Drive north from Silver City on New Mexico 15
towards Pinos Altos. At mile 26.2 is the junction with New
Mexico 35 to Lake Roberts and San Lorenzo. Bear right and
continue past Lake Roberts 12.6 miles, until the junction with
New Mexico 61 is reached. Bear left or north and continue
past North Star Mesa and Rocky Canyon Campground to
Lower Black Canyon Campground. Turn left or west into the
Campground and drive to the end of the road, which is
Trailhead 634 for the Black Canyon Trail.

The Black Canyon Trail, sometimes referred to as the Lower Black
Canyon Trail, starts at the western end of the Lower Black Canyon
Campground and continues for three miles down the canyon to the
corral. No trail exists below the corral, except perhaps a cow trail that
is not maintained and not recommended for use. Because of the
boxing-up of the canyon which occurs at this point, travel beyond the
maintained trail is very difficult on horseback and often difficult
hiking when the creek is high. This is a popular short trail into the
Wilderness for people staying at the Upper and Lower Black Canyon
campgrounds.

Crossing the North Star Road, it is possible to hike up into the
Upper Black Canyon on U.S.F.S. #72. The trail ascends Black Canyon all the way to the Continental Divide, deep within the Black

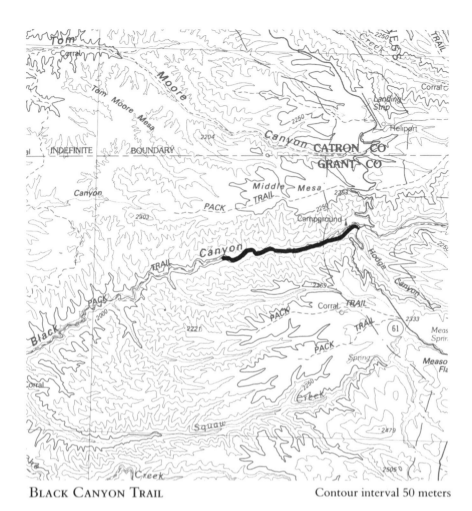

BLACK CANYON TRAIL

Contour interval 50 meters

Range. The Aldo Leopold Wilderness Area protects this region, named for the pioneering conservationist in the Forest Service who was stationed in this area early in his career and led the fight to have the Gila Wilderness designated as the nation's (and the world's) first wilderness area in 1924.

Trailhead elevation (from New Mexico 15 near Copperas
    Vista): 7,300 feet
Trail ending (near Lyons Lodge on East Fork): 5,600 feet
Total vertical ascent: 1,700 feet
Length: 6.50 miles (10.40 kilometers)
Recommended season: April through November
Use: Moderate
Difficulty: Moderate
U.S.G.S. maps: Gila Hot Springs

Access: Drive north from Silver City on New Mexico 15 past,
consecutively, Pinos Altos (mile 6.5), Ben Lilly Memorial
Marker (mile 10.4, located 150 feet west of highway), an
interesting example of columnar jointing in the Tadpole Ridge
Tuff (mile 10.8), junction with New Mexico 35 (mile 26.2),
and Copperas Vista Point (mile 33.6, elevation 7,440 feet,
finest view of the Gila Wilderness Area). Less than a mile
north of the Copperas Vista Point, on the right or east side of
the road, is the trailhead designated 643, for the Military Trail.
If you reach the sign on the right, at mile 35.1, that reads
"Downgrade next 6 miles. Use low gear," you have gone too
far.

The Military Trail is part of the old military road that originally went
from Fort Bayard north into the Gila country during cavalry days.
This trail, six and a half miles in length, goes from the piñon-juniper
country near the Copperas Vista Point to the riparian woodlands of
the East Fork of the Gila River, terminating near Lyons Lodge. It is
best taken from south to north, with someone arriving at the other
end by car to pick you up. The trail offers some very fine views of the
Gila Wilderness Area and of the Black Range Mountains to the east.
Many points of geological interest are found along the trail, as with
most trails in this area, including sandstone formations, tuff forma-

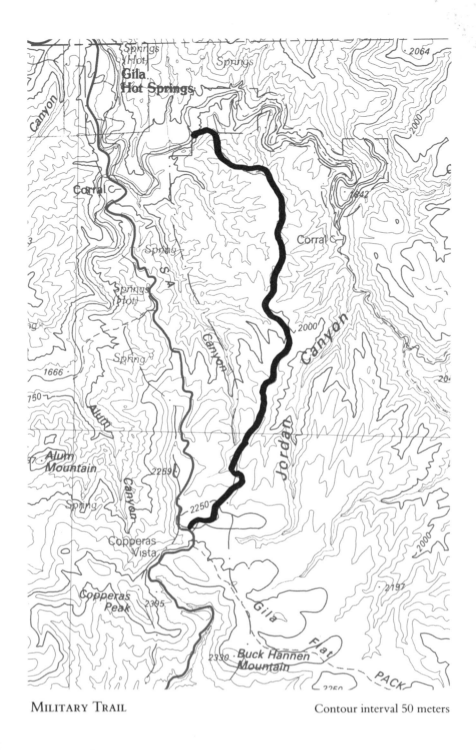

MILITARY TRAIL   Contour interval 50 meters

The eastern part of the Gila Wilderness, as seen from the old Military Trail. (Photograph by John Murray)

tions, and Gila conglomerate, an extensive blanket in the region interbedded with andesite and rhyolite flows (from the period of volcanic activity 30 to 20 million years ago). Some of these are very beautifully eroded. The Gila Hot Springs, a major geothermal water source in the area, are located near the confluence of the East and West forks at the end of the trail on private land. Water temperature is constant at about 147 degrees Fahrenheit and contains only about 414 parts per million dissolved solids but holds relatively large amounts of flourides and silica. Local residents use some of this water to heat their greenhouses.

BRANNON PARK TRAIL (U.S.F.S. #700)

Trailhead elevation (from New Mexico 35): 6,200 feet
Trail ending (Rocky Canyon Campground): 7,400 feet
Total vertical ascent: 1,200 feet
Length: 11.50 miles (18.40 kilometers)
Recommended season: April through November
Use: Moderate
Difficulty: Moderate
U.S.G.S. maps: North Star Mesa

Access: Drive north from Silver City on New Mexico 15. At mile 26.2, at the junction with New Mexico 35, bear right or east and continue past Lake Roberts along Sapillo Creek. Trailhead 640 for Brannon Park Trail #700 is located on the left or north side of the road 4.5 miles east of the Lake Roberts Shopping Center (on right side of road as you travel east). If you reach the road to the GOS ranch on the left, you have gone 2.9 miles too far.

The Brannon Park Trail is a fairly heavily used trail, and one not recommended for those seeking solitude. It is especially crowded on such holidays as Memorial Day, the Fourth of July, and Labor Day, when people fishing nearby Lake Roberts descend on the trail. Brannon Park, located 3.0 miles from Rocky Canyon Campground and 8.5 miles from Trailhead 640 on the Lake Roberts Road, is the main attraction on this trail. The park itself is an open meadow set amongst the ponderosa pine and was once the site of a frontier homestead. A careful examination along the edges of the park will locate the remains of an old rail fence that was built by the first pioneers to this area. From Sapillo Creek the trail follows Rocky Canyon for about two miles, then climbs west and then parallels it along the ridge for the rest of the distance to Brannon Park. Past Brannon Park, it winds north

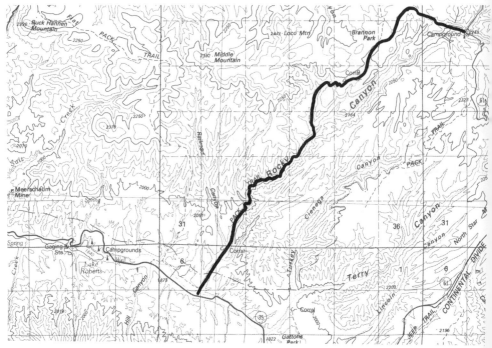

BRANNON PARK TRAIL   Contour interval 50 meters

and then east before finally rejoining Rocky Canyon a short distance
from the campground.

   Just beyond the trailhead on New Mexico 35 and over the Continental Divide is the rich agricultural valley of Mimbres. In prehistoric
times, a group of Mogollons lived in this area, known for their
beautifully designed pottery. After a persistent period of drought
between A.D. 1100 and 1200, it is thought that their agriculturally
based culture fell into a state of decline and finally collapsed. The
Apache eventually settled in the area, and, during the nineteenth
century, this branch was known as the Mimbres Apache. Their greatest chief was Mangas Coloradas, who was tortured to death at Ft.
Bayard in Pinos Altos by soldiers in 1863, thus unleashing the greatest
of all Apache war chiefs, Cochise, who waged war on the white man

relentlessly for the next ten years. Today the Mimbres Valley, well worth a side trip, is a prospering agricultural region. Deep wells drilled after World War II greatly increased the water supply. Presently, about 70,000 acres on 300 farms in the Mimbres Irrigation Basin produce cotton, milo, corn, wheat, pinto beans, and pecans, with an annual value of about $10 million. Mimbres itself is a pleasant town with several shops and stores, and a district ranger station. The ranger station is located 9.2 miles past the Brannon Park Trailhead.

[Thales] was reproached for his poverty, which was supposed to show that philosophy is of no use. According to the story, he knew by his skill [in interpreting the heavens] while it was yet winter that there would be a great harvest of olives in the coming year; so, having a little money, he gave deposits for the use of all the olive-presses in Chios and Miletus, which he hired at a low price because no one bid against him. When the harvest time came, and many were wanted all at once, he let them out at any rate which he pleased and made a quantity of money. Thus he showed the world philosophers can easily be rich if they like, but that their ambition is of another sort.

—Aristotle, *Politics* (Book I, Chapter 11, 1259a, 11–19)

West Fork of the Gila River Trail (U.S.F.S. #151)

Trailhead elevation (Gila Cliff Dwellings National
  Monument): 5,689 feet
Trail ending (Forest Road #507): 8,383 feet
Total vertical ascent: 2,694 feet
Length: 34.50 miles (55.20 kilometers)
Recommended season: April through November, except in
  periods of high water (spring runoff or flash floods)
Use: Moderate to Heavy
Difficulty: Moderate
U.S.G.S. maps: Little Turkey Park, Woodland Park, Lilley
  Mountain, Mogollon Baldy Peak, Negrito Mountain

Access: Proceed north from Silver City on New Mexico 5
towards Pinos Altos (Tall Pines). At mile 10.4 is the Ben Lilly
Memorial Marker on the left, about 150 feet west of the
highway. At mile 26.2 is the junction with New Mexico 35 to
Lake Roberts and San Lorenzo. Bear left to reach Gila Hot
Springs and the Gila Cliff Dwellings National Monument. At
mile 33.5 is the paved Copperas Vista Point, one of the finest
scenic overlooks in the Southwest. The entire heart of the Gila
Wilderness Area is visible from this point. At mile 40.9 is Gila
Hot Springs and Doc Campbell's Vacation Center, where a
small store and restaurant are located. Continue on farther,
past the turnoff to the right to the Gila Wilderness Area/Gila
Cliff Dwellings Visitor's Center, past Scorpion Campground,
to the parking area at the end of the road to the national
monument. The West Fork Trail begins at the end of the
parking lot and is clearly visible. Those with horses can park
at TJ Corral and then ride up the side trail, which skirts the
Scorpion Campground and the Cliff Dwellings. This trail is
approximately two miles long and eventually joins the river
trail on the west boundary of the monument.

The West Fork of the Gila Trail is one of the longer and more popular routes through the Gila Wilderness, particularly in the summer when the waters are low and the many river crossings (60 to 70) are easier to negotiate. Hazards common to the river canyons of the Southwest are encountered: poison ivy, rattlesnakes, quicksand, occasionally dangerous crossings in periods of high runoff, and unpredictable flash floods in the midsummer. Vegetational patterns vary along the route with respect to moisture and elevational changes. Ponderosa pine, Arizona sycamore, narrowleaf cottonwood, and Arizona alder are found in the West Fork canyon bottom, with open stands of ponderosa pine on Cub Mesa, Jack Ass Park, and Iron Creek Mesa. Douglas fir and spruce stands are found in Packsaddle Canyon, Turkeyfeather Creek, Iron Creek, and Willow Creek. Water availability is good for the entire length of the West Fork, at Turkeyfeather Spring, Iron Creek, and Iron Creek Lake. Water purification tablets or purification methods should always be used.

The first five miles of the West Fork above the cliff dwellings see perhaps more people than any other portion of the Gila Wilderness. The Grudging cabin, on the south bank, is often visited. The cliff dwelling at mile 3.1 in the rock cave above the river is a popular destination for day hikers. Many people also take this trail for a short distance to the fork with the Woodland Park–Meadows Trail, right after the second river crossing. Farther on, the trail becomes progressively less crowded, except for popular locations of high use, like the areas around Hells Hole Canyon and the confluence with White Creek. Those who seek solitude and would rather have less contact with people should use one of the other trails suggested in this book or consult with personnel at the visitor's center for areas less busy.

Numerous side canyons empty into the West Fork of the Gila River and can be used to mark your progress: Grave Canyon (2.75 miles on the right), White Rocks Canyon (3.75 miles on the left), Nat Straw Canyon (6.00 miles on the left), Ring Canyon (8.50 miles on the left), Hells Hole Canyon (12.00 miles on the right), and White Creek (15.50 miles on the left). The last 0.75 miles of trail approaching White Creek can be difficult for horses. It traverses rock slides and yielding clay along a steep embankment along the north side of the West Fork which runs loudly below in a narrow gorge with many falls and deep potholes in the rock.

From the mouth of White Creek, the trail continues along the West

The West Fork canyon, three miles into the Gila Wilderness. There is a cliff dwelling in the small cave in the lower right. (Photograph by John Murray)

Fork for another 0.50 miles before it climbs 940 feet in a series of switchbacks out onto the west flank of Cub Mesa. Here the trail continues on over Cub Mesa, turns north to cross Packsaddle Canyon into Jack Ass Park and then descends to the mouth of Cub Creek, reentering the West Fork Canyon. The trail proceeds up the West Fork for 1.25 miles and then turns right up Turkeyfeather Creek, passing Turkeyfeather Spring, and continuing up Turkeyfeather Pass. Hikers can use the West Fork Canyon from White Creek to the Cub Creek junction, but horseback riders should take the Cub Mesa Trail. From Turkeyfeather Pass, the trail descends and follows Cooper Canyon to its junction with Iron Creek. Turning up Iron Creek, the trail then follows a tributary of Iron Creek leading down from Iron Creek Lake, passes the lake, and crosses the western end of Iron Creek Mesa

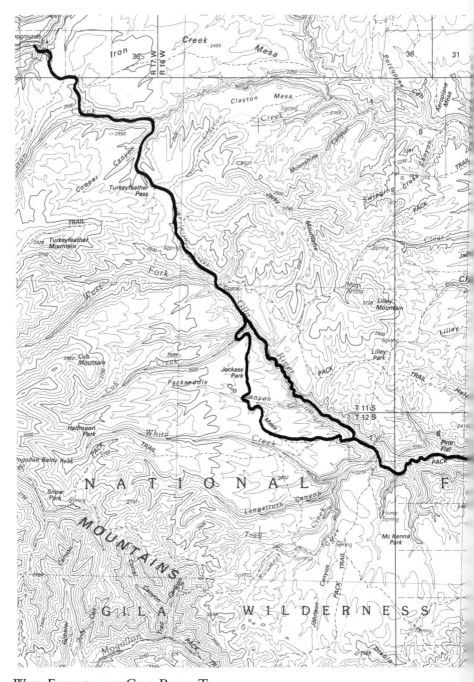

WEST FORK OF THE GILA RIVER TRAIL

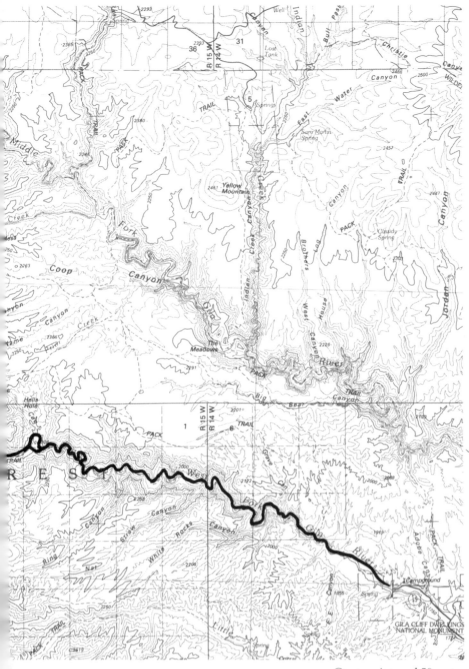

Contour interval 50 meters

and then drops into Willow Creek to its termination with a loop of Forest Road #507. Total distance is 34.50 miles and the trip can be accomplished by most hikers with someone to pick them up on the other end in three or four days.

Additionally, numerous side trails offer the hiker opportunities to explore seldom-visited parts of the Gila Wilderness. These include the following: the Turkey Creek/McKenna Park/Little Creek Trail #155, which intersects the West Fork Trail just below the mouth of White Creek; Trotter Trail #30, which goes out a half-mile above the mouth of White Creek; Mogollon Baldy Trail #152 found on Cub Mesa; Lilley Park Trail #164, Clayton Mesa Trail #175, and Turkeyfeather Trail #102, all of which are found in the vicinity of Turkeyfeather Pass; Iron Creek Mesa Trail #171, about 0.25 miles east of Iron Creek Lake; and Whitewater Baldy Trail #172 at Iron Creek Lake. Wildlife abounds both in the canyon bottoms and on the mesa tops, and the chances of seeing mule deer, elk, turkey, pine squirrels, beaver, and coyotes are usually excellent. Their tracks and sign can often be found on the trails. Fishing along the West Fork ranges from fair to excellent for trout.

MIDDLE FORK TRAIL (U.S.F.S. #157)

Trailhead elevation (near Gila Visitor's Center): 5,680 feet
Trail ending (Gilita Campground): 8,300 feet
Total vertical ascent: 2,620 feet
Length: 41.00 miles (65.60 kilometers)
Recommended season: April through November, except in
    periods of high water (spring runoff or flash floods)
Use: Moderate to heavy
Difficulty; Moderate
U.S.G.S. maps: Gila Hot Springs, Little Turkey Park, Burnt
    Corral Canyon, Woodland Park, Lilley Mountain, Loco
    Mountain, Negrito Mountain

Access: Drive north from Silver City on New Mexico 15 past,
consecutively, Pinos Altos, the Ben Lilly Memorial Marker,
Cherry Creek Campground, Mcmillan Campground,
Lookout Point, the junction with New Mexico 35, Copperas
Vista, Grapevine Campground, and Gila Hot Springs (mile
40.9). Drive past the turnoff at mile 44.0 to the Gila Cliff
Dwellings National Monument, and continue 0.3 miles to the
Gila Visitor's Center. The trailhead is located a short distance
to the north on the service road.

The Middle Fork Trail is at 41 miles the longest continuous trail in the
Gila Wilderness and one of the longest to be found in the Southwest.
In this respect, it can be compared favorably with two famous trails
farther to the north: the 80-mile long Continental Divide Trail running the crest of the divide in the Weminuche Wilderness of southern
Colorado, and the 47-mile long Thorofare–Deer Creek Trail ascending Thorofare Creek to Bridger Lake in the Teton Wilderness of
northern Wyoming. Like these trails, the Middle Fork Trail offers an
opportunity for physical challenge, solitude, and natural beauty that
has become increasingly difficult to find south of Alaska and Canada.
The trail is normally hiked when the river is low and takes from five

The Middle Fork canyon, as seen from the south rim west of the trail cut-off down into the Meadows. (Photograph by John Murray)

to seven days to complete, starting at either the Gilita Campground on Forest Service Road 78 east of Mogollon or from the Gila Visitor's Center north of Silver City.

For almost its entire length, the Middle Fork Trail remains on the bottom of the Middle Fork Canyon. In places the great barranca is over 1,000 feet deep, with beautifully intricate rock formations on its steep, eroded flanks. Rocks exposed in these regions include a thick sequence of ancient volcanic flows associated with the formation of two huge calderas (Bursum and Gila cliff dwellings) which collapsed following the expulsion of tremendous volumes of lava. Authorities believe this activity occurred about 30 to 20 million years ago. In places, the Gila conglomerate, an extensive blanket of sedimentary rock, overlaps the volcanic sequence. Formations of andesite, rhyolite, and tuff, all rocks of volcanic origin, abound in the canyons. Sometimes the tuff is found in cliff regions composed of individual, columnar joints. These polygonal joints formed in sheets as the material cooled and then contracted soon after being deposited. The jointing process is analogous to that observed in mud banks drying under a hot sun.

The riparian deciduous forests found along the canyon bottoms are typical of those in the Southwest. Predominant trees include the sycamore, walnut, ash, maple, willow, cottonwood, and alder. Vines include the wild grape and Virginia creeper. In such places as the popular Meadows region, ponderosa pine trees form large, stable communities on the canyon floor. The enormous size of some of these specimens—diameters exceeding 2 feet and heights well over 100 feet—attests to the enduring nature of these groves. Birdlife abounds in these woodlands. Most of the north-facing slopes along the canyon are, where not covered with exposed rock, vegetated with ponderosa pine. South-facing slopes are covered with piñon-juniper woodland and large grassy areas.

There are, on average, 3 river crossings per linear mile of trail, with over 100 crossings along the entire length of the trail. In most areas, hikers will have long stretches of cobblestone or soft sand to walk on. Quicksand is sometimes found in wet areas along the river. These river crossings are in places impossible to make during periods of high water. Because of fluctuating river levels, combined with frequent periods of flooding, in most cases an obvious trail will not make itself

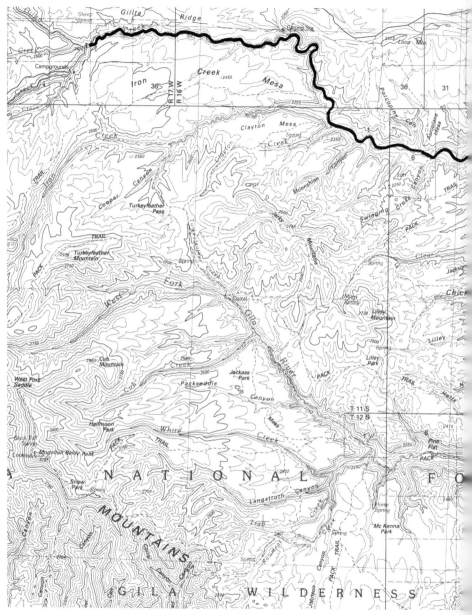

MIDDLE FORK TRAIL

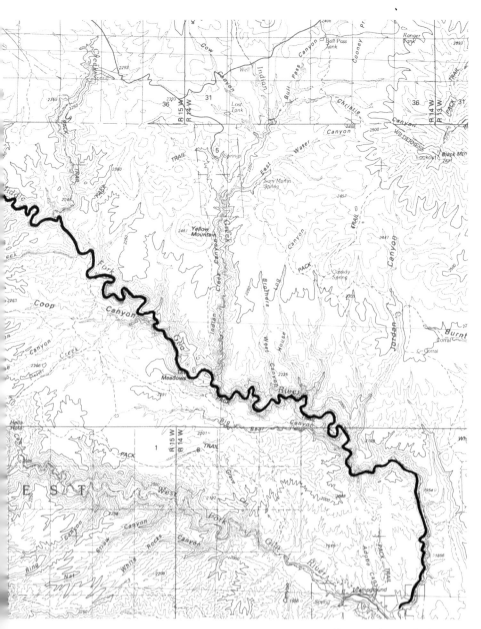

Contour interval 50 meters

apparent along the river bottom. Hikers searching for the trail in these heavily wooded regions should be alert for poison ivy and rattlesnakes. Excellent fishing is found along many areas of this route year-round. Because of its lower elevations, portions of the Middle Fork Trail provide a good cool weather trail as well. In places, remnant cliff dwellings can be seen in the natural caves located in the canyon.

Important trails and features located along the Middle Fork Trail which can be used to plot your progress are as follows, with mileages from the Gilita Campground in the event you start there: Snow Canyon Trail #142 (6.00 miles), Iron Creek Trail #171 (9.00 miles), Clayton Creek Trail #175 (10.00 miles), Swinging Cross Canyon Trail #30 (12.00 miles), Flying V Canyon Trail #706 (13.50 miles), Canyon Creek Trail #31 (17.25 miles), Clear Creek Canyon (no trail—18.50 miles), Chicken Coop Canyon (no trail—24.00 miles), the Meadows Trail #28 (26.00 miles), Jordon Canyon (no trail—33.00 miles), Big Bear Canyon (no trail—33.50 miles), Little Bear Canyon Trail #729 (34.50 miles), and North Mesa Trail #27 (38.00 miles).

A trip down or up the Middle Fork is a journey into the heart of a magnificent wilderness, a sometimes lonely and austere place such as Christ and the prophets went out into, a place from which you emerge with a renewed commitment to life and mankind. From the fragile pasque flowers of the April hillsides to the towering ponderosa pines of the meadows, it is a place rich in the natural poetry of the earth. Two miles from the Gila Visitor's Center you can sit in the same hot springs that were used by Geronimo, Mangas Coloradas, Victorio, Cochise, and all those who came before them. You can look up at the same stars, and hear the same peaceful river, and wonder the same things. The wilderness is a good place to rediscover the sense of wonder we all had as children, and without which life is a very dull affair indeed. There are few better places to accomplish this in the Southwest than the Middle Fork Trail.

GILA RIVER TRAIL* (U.S.F.S. #724)

Trailhead elevation (near Grapevine Campground): 5,300 feet
Trail ending (near Turkey Creek): 4,770 feet
Total vertical ascent: 530 feet
Length: 32.50 miles (51.20 kilometers)
Recommended season: April through November, except in
  periods of high water (spring runoff or flash floods)
Use: Moderate to heavy
Difficulty: Moderate
U.S.G.S. maps: Gila Hot Springs, Granny Mountain, Canyon
  Hill, Canteen Canyon

Access: Drive north from Silver City on New Mexico 15 past,
consecutively, Pinos Altos, the Ben Lilly Memorial Marker,
Cherry Creek Campground, McMillan Campground,
Lookout Point, the junction with New Mexico 35, and
Copperas Vista. The Gila River Trail begins at the Upper Gila
River Bridge (mile 39.5) just below the confluence of the East
and West forks, across the road from the Grapevine
Campground. If you reach Gila Hot Springs (mile 40.9) you
have gone too far.

*The Gila River Trail is in the Wilderness District for the first 7 miles and in
the Silver City District for the last 25 miles.

The Gila River Trail is similar in many respects to the Middle Fork
and West Fork trails. It is, like them, a river bottom trail involving
many crossings. Often an obvious trail will not be found, and hiking
is for the most part over long stretches of cobblestone and soft sand,
interspersed with riparian forest and grassy meadows. The Gila Canyon, like that of its two major tributaries upstream, ranges in width
from fairly narrow to moderately wide, with the river course mean-
dering back and forth across the small valley and often changing
course after storms. Warm and hot springs are found periodically

The Gila River, as seen from the ridge north of the Copperas Vista pull-out. (Photograph by John Murray)

along its length, with two of the most popular at Turkey Creek 32.00 miles downstream and near the Grapevine Trailhead 1.75 miles downstream. There is an abundance of natural caves in the rock of the canyon sides with cliff dwellings in evidence at points. North-facing slopes are vegetated with ponderosa pine. South-facing slopes are covered with piñon-juniper woodland and grassy areas. The familiar water-loving sycamore-cottonwood complex dominates the river bottom. Some excellent fishing for catfish, trout, and bass can be found on the river. Side canyons offer hunting for deer, bear, and other species in season.

The Gila River is one of the few rivers in the Southwest which can be floated in the spring, just as such rivers as the Dolores, Colorado, Green, and Yampa are farther north. Many groups, such as the Sierra Club, either sponsor or outfit such trips, generally made in the early spring when the runoff is highest. Such trips normally take five to seven days to run the entire length of the river, from the Grapevine Campground Area to Mogollon Creek with side trips to various points of interest, such as Indian ruins and hot springs. Whitewater enthusiasts consider the Gila a Class III river, offering rapids that challenge most intermediate boaters while being too much for the novice and too little for the expert. In Class III rapids, boaters encounter challenging waves and holes, formidable rocks that must be avoided, and places where decisions have to be made about which line or channel to take. Rafters, canoeists, and kayakers can all find serious fun on the Gila River. A trip down a river is something all outdoor enthusiasts should try at least once in their lives. From the Noatak Wild River in the high arctic of Alaska to the Gila River in the desert uplands of New Mexico, America is blessed with some very beautiful rivers that are still as wild as when the Pilgrims first arrived on the continent. Hopefully, the Gila will not be dammed as some would like to see. Muir once compared the damming of his beloved Hetch Hetchy Valley in the Sierras to the damming of a great cathedral. The same might be said of the canyon of the Gila, holding as it does not only areas of great natural beauty but also a virtual museum of man's history in the region, from cliff dwellings to petroglyphs to pioneer sites.

Important trails and features located along the Gila River Trail which can be used to plot your progress are as follows with mileages from the Grapevine Campground Trailhead: Alum Camp Trail #788 (1.00 mile), Hot Springs (1.75 miles), Granny Mountain Trail #160 (13.00 miles), Spring Canyon Trail #247 (Sapillo Creek Confluence—15.25 miles), Sheep Corral Canyon Trail #231 (trailhead on Sapillo Creek, 0.25 miles east of river—6.00 miles to Sheep Corral and Forest Road 282), Panther Canyon Trail #254 (17.00 miles), Packsaddle Canyon Trail #732 (21.00 miles), Water Canyon (no trail—21.50 miles), Hells Canyon (no trail—23.00 miles), Utah Bill Canyon (no trail—27.00 miles), Hidden Pasture Canyon (no trail—30.00 miles), and Turkey Creek (32.00 miles).

Spring floaters on the Gila and hikers as well should remember that once beginning down or upstream, it is 15 (or 17) miles to the nearest wilderness exit—Spring Canyon or Sheep Corral Canyon, respectively. Persons traveling in these isolated regions should be well prepared for emergencies that can quickly arise in primitive situations.

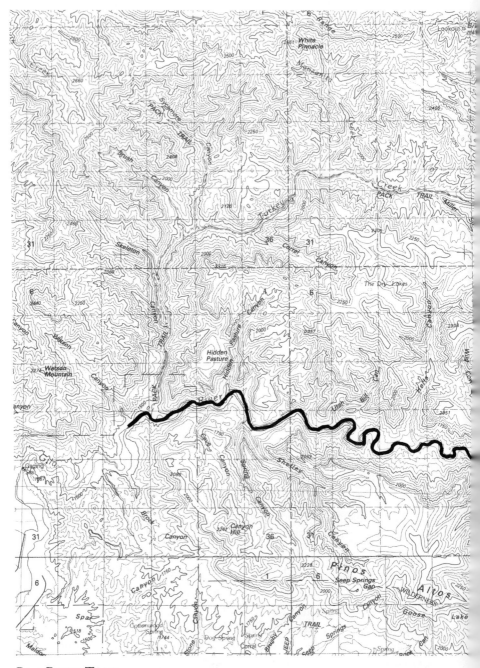

GILA RIVER TRAIL

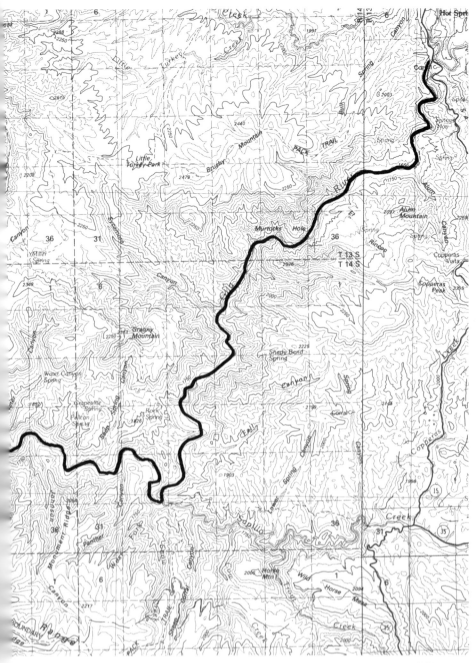

Contour interval 50 meters

As with the other river trails, sneakers or running shoes should be carried for the many river crossings. Portages are in place around the wire water-gap fences, and the wire should of course not be cut. Cattle are occasionally encountered along the river and all gates passed through should be properly secured.

The Gila River Trail passes through one of the more historic regions in the Southwest. On the canyon walls, ancient images of deer and the men who hunted them are visible. The clay, mud, and stone cliff dwellings and storage caves of these same people are found up and down the river. Occasionally, someone finds an Apache arrowhead in the gravel beside the river or the spent shell casing of a cavalry rifle, attesting to more recent history. In the morning, hikers often find the cloven tracks of mule deer on the sand, and sometimes the soft imprints of a mountain lion beside them. At night the coyotes call back and forth across the canyon rims, and the stars twinkle between them. Something more than a canyon will be lost if the Gila River is ever dammed. A bit of our freedom will have drowned with it.

GRANNY MOUNTAIN TRAIL (U.S.F.S. #160)

Trailhead elevation (Woody's Corral): 5,670 feet
Trail ending (Gila River): 5,100 feet
Total vertical ascent (high point of 7,650 feet): 1,980 feet
Length: 20.50 miles (32.80 kilometers)
Use: Light to moderate
Difficulty: Moderate to difficult
U.S.G.S. maps: Little Turkey Park, Granny Mountain

Access: Drive north from Silver City on New Mexico 15 past, consecutively, Pinos Altos, the junction with New Mexico 35, Copperas Vista, and Gila Hot Springs (mile 40.9). At mile 44.0 turn left or northwest on the road to the Gila Cliff Dwellings National Monument. TJ Trailhead Corral is found at mile 45.3 on the right. Little Creek Trailhead is located just south of the West Fork Bridge at an old corral across the road from the TJ Corral. This corral, where the Little Creek Trail begins, is known as Woody's Corral. If you reach the Scorpion Campground on the north or right side of the road at mile 45.6, you have gone too far.

The Granny Mountain Trail, running from Woody's Corral on the West Fork south for 20.5 miles to the Gila River, is for the most part not heavily used and can be suggested as a good route for hikers seeking solitude in the less visited regions of the Gila Wilderness. The vegetation encountered is representative of that found in the Wilderness as a whole: piñon-juniper on the south-facing slopes, ponderosa pine on the north-facing slopes, some deciduous riparian communities, grasslands, and oak woodlands. Wildlife is plentiful. Water is scarce for much of the trail and should be carried by hikers.

The trail climbs south and west from Woody's Corral, following the north ridge of a side canyon to the West Fork. At mile 3.5 the trail begins to gradually descend down a side canyon towards Little Creek, reaching it at mile 4.0. After crossing Little Creek, the trail continues south and west, passing over Little Turkey Creek at mile 5.2 and reaching Little Turkey Park itself at mile 7.3. At the juncture with the Brushy Mountain Trail (U.S.F.S. #403), turn right or west and follow the Granny Mountain Trail as it skirts the rim of Sycamore Canyon, which drains into the Gila River. At mile 12.8 Miller Springs is reached, located at the head of Miller Spring Canyon which drains into Turkey Creek, a short distance to the north and west. Turn left or south at the junction with the Miller Spring Trail, and continue 7.5 miles past Granny Mountain to the left or east to the end of the Granny Mountain Trail at the bottom of the Gila Canyon reached at mile 20.3. It is 13.0 miles upstream at this point to New Mexico 15 and the beginning of the Gila River Trail (U.S.F.S. #724).

A popular loop trail in the Gila Wilderness is to take the Granny Mountain Trail to Miller Spring, pick up the interconnecting Miller Spring Trail (U.S.F.S. #159) over to the Turkey Creek Trail (U.S.F.S. #155), and then follow the Turkey Creek Trail over to the Little Creek Spring, at which point Little Creek can be followed (Little Creek Trail—U.S.F.S. #161), back down to the Granny Mountain Trail (U.S.F.S. #160) and to Woody's Corral. The total length of this three- to five-day backcountry trip is 34.5 miles (55.2) kilometers, offering a grand tour and a convenient circuit route through a very scenic and isolated portion of the Gila Wilderness.

Water is scarce in this region and along the Granny Mountain Trail can normally be found at the following locations: the Little Creek junction except during the very driest times of the year, the Little Turkey Creek junction in times of heavy rainfall or runoff, Miller Spring, and the Gila River. The water at the Little Turkey Park Tank is muddy. There will possibly be water in the Brushy Mountain area in the wet season. Clear water can always be found down on Turkey Creek and at Miller Spring.

Oak trees are found periodically along this trail. These are important trees in the ecosystem, for they, like piñon trees, provide a bountiful food source in the woodlands. The acorns are consumed by diverse species from squirrels and rabbits to jays and magpies to raccoons and bears. A common bird encountered along this trail is the wild turkey. Their gobbling call, similar to that of domestic turkeys, is often heard by hikers and campers in this area. The males have a bluish, naked head with red wattles that brighten during the spring

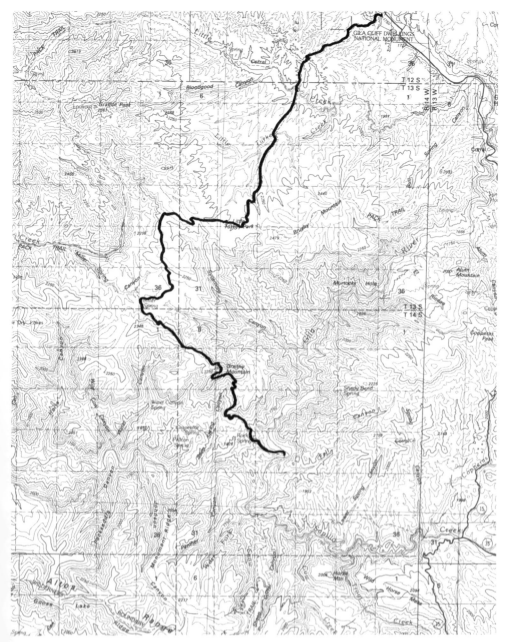

GRANNY MOUNTAIN TRAIL   Contour interval 50 meters

The crossing at Little Creek on the trail to Granny Mountain. (Photograph by John Murray)

courtship rituals. The body is dusky brown with a bronzy iridescent sheen to it in the sun. In courtship the male spreads its tawny tail in a fan, revealing a broad black subterminal band with a white or buffy edge. The male also has spurs on its legs and a long dangling tuft of feathers, called the beard, in the middle of the breast. Females, which are considerably smaller, less iridescent, and frequently lack a beard, are gathered into harems by the older breeding males in the spring. This process of males fighting among themselves for the right to breed the females is similar to that observed in the elk, with their bugling challenges and jousting matches in the autumn. The gobbling of the turkeys in any season can make it difficult for campers to obtain sufficient sleep on the Granny Mountain Trail and similar trails through turkey country. Attempts to quiet them on nights when they are particularly obnoxious (as under a full moon) usually result in increased gobbling and bruised shins from running through the half-lit woods after them.

PRIOR CABIN TRAIL (U.S.F.S. #156)

Trailhead elevation (junction with U.S.F.S. #164): 7,320 feet
Trail ending (junction with U.S.F.S. #28): 6,920 feet
Total vertical ascent: 400 feet
Length: 5.50 miles (8.80 kilometers)
Recommended season: April through November (Snows
    sometimes close the trail early or linger into the spring)
Use: Moderate
Difficulty: Moderate
U.S.G.S. maps: Lilley Mountain, Woodland Park

Access: This trail is located in the interior of the Gila
Wilderness. Access is from U.S.F.S. #164 (See Lilley Park
Trail description) on the west and from U.S.F.S. #28 (See
Meadows Trail description) on the east.

The Prior Cabin Trail (see "A Guide to Wilderness Places Names" in
the appendix) provides access from the rim of the Middle Fork Canyon to the vicinity of Prior Cabin overlooking Hells Hole on the West
Fork Canyon. The trail is 5.5 miles long and begins near the head of
Prior Creek on the Lilley Park Trail. It follows Prior Creek down to
the actual site of Prior Cabin (2.25 miles), and then turns east gradually climbing out of Prior Creek. It follows a flat ridgetop between the
Middle Fork and Big Bear Canyon to the termination of the trail at
the junction with Big Bear Trail #28. Predominant vegetation along
the trail is ponderosa pine, with wildlife such as turkey, deer, and elk
sometimes encountered. Prior Creek usually runs water intermit-
tently in all but the driest months of the year. Water is also available
from a spring just below the Chicken Coop Trail intersection (just 25
feet to the right of the creek bottom). Chicken Coop Trail #29 makes
contact with the Prior Cabin Trail in the proximity of Prior Cabin,
2.25 miles from the junction with the Lilley Park Trail. One-half mile
farther east, the Woodland Park Trail (U.S.F.S. #12) intersects the
Prior Cabin Trail.

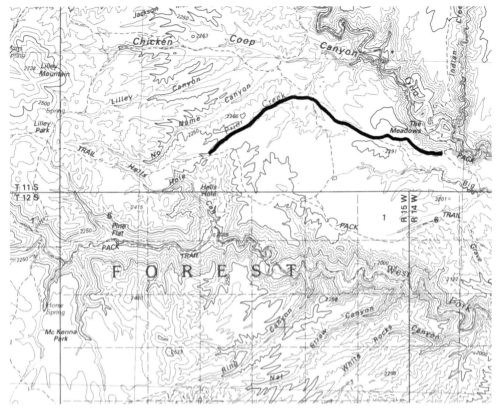

PRIOR CABIN TRAIL   Contour interval 50 meters

LITTLE BEAR TRAIL (U.S.F.S. #729)

Trailhead elevation (near Scorpion Corral Campground):
  5,670 feet
Trail ending (Middle Fork): 5,880 feet
Total vertical ascent (high point of 6,380 feet): 710 feet
Length: 4.00 miles (6.40 kilometers)
Recommended season: April through November
Use: Heavy
Difficulty: Moderate
U.S.G.S. maps: Little Turkey Park, Woodland Park

Access: Drive north from Silver City on New Mexico 15 past,
consecutively, Pinos Altos, the junction with New Mexico 35,
Copperas Vista, and Gila Hot Springs (mile 40.9). At mile 44.0
turn left or northwest on the road to the Gila Cliff Dwellings
National Monument. TJ Trailhead Corral is found at mile 45.3
on the right. Little Bear Trailhead is on the north side of the
corral. If you reach the Scorpion Campground on the north or
right side of the road at mile 45.6, you have gone too far.

The Little Bear Trail, which connects the West Fork with the Middle
Fork by way of Little Bear Canyon, is one of the more popular and
heavily used trails in the Gila Wilderness. It is used to reach the
Meadows, located on the Middle Fork, as well as fishing and thermal
sites on the lower Middle Fork. The trail in this respect is not recommended for those desiring solitude in the backcountry. It would be a
good trail for those seeking an interesting day hike into the peripheral
regions of the Two Forks country, which ranges all the way from the
confluence near the Gila Visitor's Center to Lilley Mountain, in the
vicinity of the Mogollon Mountains, midway between the headwaters of the West and Middle forks.

Beginning at TJ Corral, the trail gradually ascends an open piñon-
juniper slope, following a local ridge system to a high point just above
the Little Bear Canyon. Mule deer can be seen throughout the entire

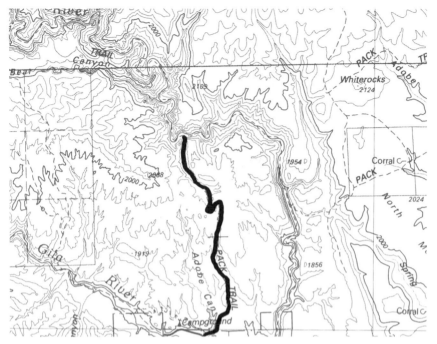

LITTLE BEAR TRAIL   Contour interval 50 meters

length of this trail, particularly in the morning and around the evening hours. Their tracks will probably be more numerous on the trail
than those of the hikers. After reaching the high point, the trail drops
down into a side canyon of Little Bear, descends a little farther, picks
up the main canyon (mile 2.75), and then follows it to the Middle
Fork of the Gila River and the Middle Fork Trail #157. The last 0.5
miles of the Little Bear Trail passes through a deep narrow gorge that
is seldom more than 45 feet wide. During periods of heavy rainfall,
this area will see flooding. Caution should be exercised in this regard
while hiking this and other trails in narrow canyons. There is a small
spring just before the canyon opens up on the Middle Fork.

The Middle Fork Trail, like the other river bottom trails, is maintained. Frequent river changes and flooding prevent the maintenance
of permanent river crossings. Hikers along the river must be prepared

for numerous river crossings, sometimes as many as six per linear mile. During periods of heavy runoff and seasonal flooding, these crossings are often impossible on foot and sometimes even dangerous with a horse. Along the Middle Fork in this area, there are two small hot springs. The first is located about a half-mile up the river above the Gila Visitor's Center, on the north side of the river near a conspicuous natural rock cave. Two crossings must be made from the visitor's center to reach this site. The second is located about two miles, or 14 river crossings, above the junction of the Little Bear Trail and the Middle Fork Trail. Fishing is often good in this part of the Gila Wilderness. The Little Bear Trail is also used by many hikers for access to the Woodland Park–Lilley Park Trail (U.S.F.S. #164).

MEADOWS TRAIL (U.S.G.S. #151 and U.S.F.S. 28)

Trailhead elevation (Gila Cliff Dwellings National
  Monument): 5,689 feet
Trail ending (Meadows): 6,420 feet
Total vertical ascent (high point of 7,120 feet): 1,431 feet
Length: 9.00 miles (14.40 kilometers)
Recommended season: April through November
Use: Moderate to heavy
Difficulty: Moderate
U.S.G.S. maps: Little Turkey Park, Woodland Park

Access: Drive north from Silver City on New Mexico 15 past,
consecutively, Pinos Altos, the Ben Lilly Memorial Marker,
Cherry Creek Campground, McMillan Campground,
Lookout Point, the junction with New Mexico 35, Copperas
Vista, Grapevine Campground, and Gila Hot Springs. Turn
left at mile 44.0 on the road to the Gila Cliff Dwellings. Stop
at the parking lot (mile 45.3). West Fork Trailhead, preferred
access, is located at the west end of the parking lot. Alternative
access, if the river is too high to cross, is from Little Bear
Canyon (see Little Bear Trail description). Just before that trail
(#729) drops down into Little Bear Canyon, the junction with
the Woodland Park–Lilly Park trail is reached. About three
miles west of this point, the junction with U.S.F.S. #28 is
reached as it approaches Big Bear Canyon en route to the
Meadows.

The Meadows Trail is one of the more popular trails in the Two Forks
country, leading to one of the most lovely regions along the Middle
Fork River. The distance is not overly great for most people—9.0
miles—and the hike generally takes about half a day (averaging 2.5 to
3.0 miles per hour). For this reason, it is a favorite of those with a long
weekend to spend in the Gila Wilderness (one day in, one day there,

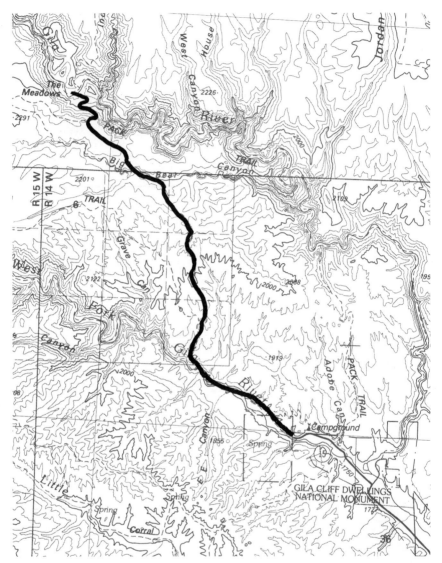

MEADOWS TRAIL   Contour interval 50 meters

one day out) and probably should be avoided at that time. It is not a trail to be recommended for those seeking solitude (except in the early spring and late fall when few, if any, people are there), but a good trail for those who want to see a beautiful place and don't care who is there with them. If you like a crowd (and some do), the Meadows is a good place to go.

The trail makes three stream crossings before reaching the Zig Zag Trail (#28). The Grudging Cabin (see "A Guide to Wilderness Place Names" in the appendix) is located on the south bank in this region. The last crossing can be difficult in times of high water because the river is constricted through a narrow place at this point. Alternative crossings upstream can be safer and should be sought if the water appears even remotely hazardous. Generally this is true only in the spring during the snow runoff. Other times it poses no problem. The Zig Zag Trail, a former stock driveway for cattle during the 1880s, can be a little steep in places. It will take about 45 minutes to reach the top of the canyon, and the view there is quite nice, but nothing compared to what you will see on the south rim of the Middle Fork Canyon in a few hours. About three miles from the West Fork, the trail reaches its junction with the Woodland Park–Lilley Park Trail, intersecting it from east to west. The trail ascends a small ridgeline of 7,120 feet, descends into the headwaters of Big Bear Canyon, gently climbs out, intersects Trail #156 on the left (see Prior Cabin Trail description), and then winds over to the rim of the West Fork Canyon.

You see its light, glowing up from the edge of the dark earth, and sense its vast emptiness even before you reach the side. And then suddenly you are there, peering carefully over the edge into a prodigious 1,000-foot abyss, carved by a great river given eons to do its job. The trail down into the Meadows is quite steep at first but eventually finds a good grade. There is one crossing over the West Fork at the bottom where the river is wide, and there are many good camping places in the grassy meadows and magnificent groves of enormous ponderosa pine trees. Fishing is good down and upstream from the Meadows, particularly where the warm springs drain into the river on the downstream side. Don't keep any fish you aren't going to eat, and carefully return all fish you aren't going to keep to

The Meadows on the Middle Fork, as seen from the south rim of the canyon. Black Mountain is visible in the upper right of the photograph. (Photograph by John Murray)

the water. Because of heavy use, it is also important to keep a clean campsite and police the area before you leave. The Meadows is one of those places that won't disappoint you. The only problem is how to fit the view from the canyon rim into one picture—a wide-angle lens is the only way.

Woodland Park–Lilley Park Trail (U.S.F.S. #164)

Trailhead elevation (Gila Cliff Dwellings National
  Monument): 5,689 feet
Trail ending (White Creek on West Fork): 6,920 feet
Total vertical ascent (high point of 8,020 feet): 2,331 feet
Length (to White Creek): 22.00 miles (35.20 kilometers)
Recommended season: April through November
Use: Moderate
Difficulty: Moderate
U.S.G.S. maps: Little Turkey Park, Woodland Park, Lilley
  Mountain, Diablo Range

Access: This trail is located in the interior of the Gila
Wilderness. Access is from U.S.F.S. #28 and #729 (see
respective trail descriptions for Meadows Trail and Little Bear
Trail) on the east side, and from the West Fork Trail #151 on
the west (see trail description for West Fork Trail), as well as
numerous spur trails in the vicinity. Trail actually ends at
Turkeyfeather Pass in the Jerky Mountains, although this trail
description takes it only as far as Lilley Park and White Creek
down below.

This trail provides access to a variety of interesting and historic places
in the Two Forks country: Woodland Park, Prior Creek, Hells Hole
Canyon, Lilley Park, and, finally, the confluence of White Creek and
the West Fork. It is pretty much an uphill climb all the way to Lilley
Park, with the steepest part of from the Zig Zag Trail on the West
Fork if that approach is used. The longer, but gentler ascent (at first),
is via the Little Bear Trail above TJ Corral (for both of these, see their
respective trail descriptions). Vegetative types include piñon-juniper,
ponderosa, and open, rolling terrain. Mule deer are normally seen and
elk are sometimes observed in the broad interstream uplands between
the two rivers.

  Assuming one begins, as most do, from the Zig Zag Trail (route to the Meadows), the trail proceeds west past the headwaters of Grave Canyon (draining south towards West Fork), where there is a small muddy tank. Three miles west of that tank, in the headwaters of Big Bear Creek, is another small muddy tank. Two miles farther west, on the right, is Trail #12, which leads across Woodland Park to the Prior Creek Trail (#156). About one and a half miles beyond this point is Trail #268, which descends in a series of switchbacks into Hells Hole Canyon on the West Fork. The switchbacks were reconstructed in 1983 and 1984. Fishing can be good at this location, although the climb back out is long and hard. About a mile past Trail #268, on the right or north side of the trail, is the Prior Cabin Trail. Downstream on Prior Creek water can be found in all but the driest months of the year, one of the few locations near this trail where good water can be found. The trail then skirts the south rim of No Name Canyon for several miles before reaching Lilley Park. Lilley Park Spring is about one mile north on Trail #30 on the southeast side of Lilley Mountain. Hikers should return to the juncture of #164 and #30 and head south on #30 two miles to the confluence of White Creek and the West Fork. The trail down into the canyon is very steep and difficult at times. Trail #164 actually continues farther west, to Turkeyfeather Pass in the Jerky Mountains. This segment, along with Trail #268 into Hells Hole and the West Fork above the White Creek confluence, are dangerous for livestock travel, if not impossible.

Even a cursory reading of the "Guide to Wilderness Place Names" found in the appendix of this book will inform the reader as to the fascinating and sometimes lively history of this part of the Wilderness. A history of Lilley Park or the White Creek confluence reads like the script of an exciting western movie and probably could provide several stories for one. It was here that the first wilderness ranger, Henry Woodrow, naturally gravitated when he was sent into the area on May 16, 1909. His sole instructions were "to go up there and look out for fires and put them out." All he had were two horses, food supplies, and an axe and a shovel. No tent was furnished. He simply used an extra tarp when it rained. He chose as his headquarters the beautiful, centrally located meadows where White Creek joins the West Fork. From here he could patrol all the fishing streams and sheep camps in the area from Turkey Creek and Mogollon Creek to Lilley Mountain and Mogollon Baldy and farther. Few trails were available

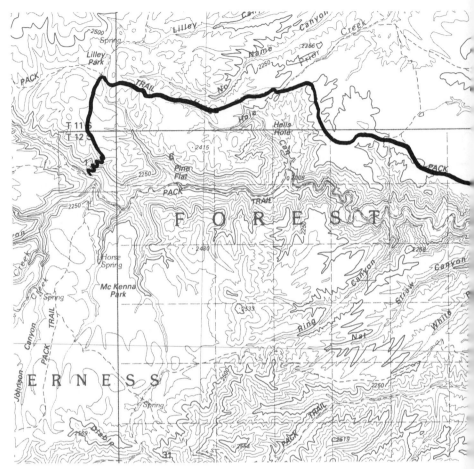

WOODLAND PARK–LILLEY PARK TRAIL

back then. Woodrow often had to blaze his own trails into the Wilderness, trails such as we use today, trails such as the Woodland Park–Lilley Park Trail. Eventually, at the age of 32, he "raised up courage enough" to marry a widowed woman in Gila and brought her up to his summer camp on White Creek where he had constructed a modest cabin. As the years passed, he was given increasing responsibilities and assistance, including fire lookouts and trail crews. This was the

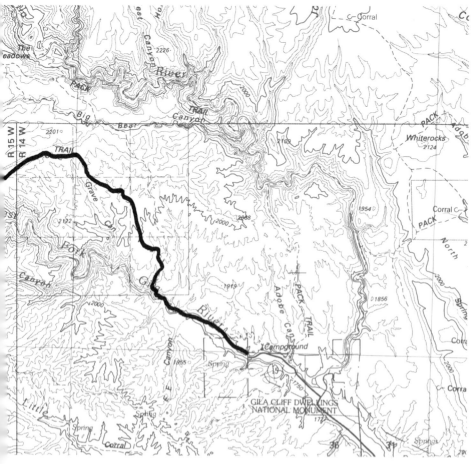

Contour interval 50 meters

rudimentary beginning of the modern Forest Service management in this vast wild area. Many other historic figures visited or hunted in the White Creek area: Ben Lilly, Nat Straw, Bear Moore, Prior, Papenoe, the McKenzie Brothers, Ralph Jenks, and the great Aldo Leopold, who founded the concept of wilderness. Today the Wilderness is much as these first pioneers found it, a place of hardship, risk, and challenge. Names like Grave Canyon, Prior Creek, and Raw Meat

The trail to Lilley Park above Hell's Hole Canyon. Ponderosa pine stands dominate in this area. (Photograph by John Murray)

Canyon all have tales behind them left by the early explorers. The Gila Wilderness today still offers an area where the adventurous may go and return with their own tales, some of them as tall as those of their forefathers. The Woodland Park–Lilley Park Trail sees light to moderate use beyond Hells Hole and offers an excellent opportunity to experience the core of this pristine wilderness. Water is scarce, but if it is carried and carefully rationed, its absence should be no obstacle to exploring this region. After the many long, hot, and dry miles, it is indeed a rare pleasure to watch the beavers superintend their dams on White Creek and the West Fork and listen to the red-winged black-birds warble from their cattail roosts. They wear their bright red wing epaulets as proudly as generals and defend their territory as vigorously, if only with a song: "Ok-a-lee! Ok-a-lee!"

Ring Canyon Trail (U.S.F.S. #162)

Trailhead elevation (Woody's Corral): 5,670 feet
Trail ending (McKenna Spring): 7,680 feet
Total vertical ascent (high point of 7,890 feet): 2,220 feet
Length: 17.00 miles (27.20 kilometers)
Recommended season: April through November
Use: Light to moderate
Difficulty: Moderate
U.S.G.S. maps: Little Turkey park, Diablo Range

Access: Drive north from Silver City on New Mexico 15 past, consecutively, Pinos Altos, the junction with New Mexico 35, Copperas Vista, and Gila Hot Springs (mile 40.9). At mile 44.0 turn left or northwest on the road to the Gila Cliff Dwellings National Monument. TJ Trailhead Corral is found at mile 45.3 on the right. Little Creek (McKenna Park) Trailhead is located just south of the West Fork Bridge at an old corral across the road from the TJ Corral. This corral, where the Little Creek (McKenna Park) Trail begins, is known as Woody's Corral. If you reach the Scorpion Campground on the north or right side of the road at mile 45.6, you have gone too far.

To reach the Ring Canyon Trail, you must first take the Granny Mountain Trail #160 (see Granny Mountain Trail description). This trail climbs southwest from Woody's Corral, following the north ridge of a side canyon to the West Fork. At mile 3.5, before the trail begins to go down a side canyon towards Little Creek, you reach the juncture on the west or right as you face south with the Ring Canyon Trail. This trail keeps to the 7,000-foot ridge to the north of Little Creek, with White Rocks Canyon, Nat Straw Canyon, and Ring Canyon in that order appearing to the north of the trail. At the southern edges of McKenna Park, the trail turns left, crosses Mc Kenna Creek, and then follows it to McKenna Spring, located just above where Trail #162 is bisected by Trail #155 (which can be used as a

Black Mountain, in the far distance, as seen from the McKenna Park Trail. (Photograph by John Murray)

spur trail to reach Little Creek Spring four miles to the south and White Creek five miles to the north).

Total distance to McKenna Springs is 17.0 miles (27.2 kilometers), a good two-day hike. The springs are often muddy. Vegetation encountered along the way include the familiar piñon-juniper association, grassy ponderosa stands, oak and walnut associations, and grasslands. This trail would be an alternative route, together with the West Fork Trail and the Woodland Park–Lilley Park Trail, to the White Creek confluence with the West Fork by way of Trail #155.

The high pastures of McKenna Park, and other areas like it in the Gila Wilderness, are good places to sit down with your binoculars or spotting scope and watch the wildlife. In the early morning and evening hours, deer are often seen, browsing through the forage. Both the mule deer and the white-tailed deer can be seen. Coyotes are found, too, and are particularly fun to watch if they are unaware of

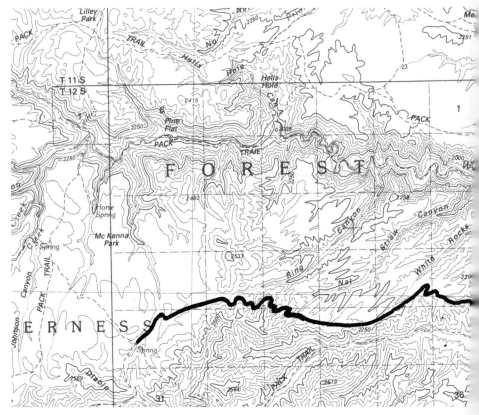

RING CANYON TRAIL

your presence. Usually by July they have taken their pups from the whelping den and are out and about with them, teaching them how to hunt and survive. They live on just about anything they can find from grasshoppers and lizards to mice and wood rats. Sometimes they eat grass, apparently to scour the ringworms and tapeworms that chronically infest their intestines. The coyote, like its larger relative the wolf, lives in a social world—the pack—normally consisting of an alpha male, an alpha female, their offspring, and perhaps a few older siblings or cousins. An invisible pecking order is maintained in this

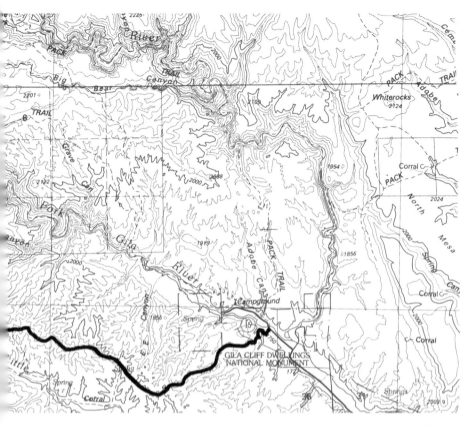

Contour interval 50 meters

little society through a variety of behavioral expressions, a kind of primitive body language. The social ordering is not as well defined in the coyote society as in the wolf society. Once wolves roamed throughout the Gila. By the 1930s they had all been exterminated. Perhaps one day the wolf will be reintroduced into the area, pursuing like the coyote its unique system of free enterprise, stirring visitors with its deep, mesmerizing howl, and husbanding as it did for tens of thousands of years before steel traps and strychnine the dependent herds of grazing animals. In many places in the world, from the suburbs of Fairbanks to the Appenine Mountains near Rome, the wolf has proven it can peacefully coexist with modern man. It has been 50 winters since a wolf left his track on the snow of McKenna Park or howled to the moon as it rose over the Black Range. It is not too late to put him back, like a priceless work of art stolen from a museum, where he rightfully belongs for all to behold.

Sycamore Canyon–Woodrow Canyon Trail (U.S.F.S. #158)

Trailhead elevation (Turkey Creek): 5,440 feet
Trail ending (Mogollon Creek): 7,040 feet
Total vertical ascent (high point of 8,000 feet): 2,560 feet
Length: 6.00 miles (9.60 kilometers)
Recommended season: April through November, except in
   periods of high water (spring runoff or flash floods)
Use: Light
Difficulty: Moderate
U.S.G.S. maps: Shelley Peak, Diablo Range

Access: This trail is located in the interior of the Gila
Wilderness. Access is from U.S.F.S. #155 (see Turkey Creek
Trail description) on the south and from U.S.F.S. #153 (see 74
Mountain–Mogollon Creek Trail description) on the north.

The Sycamore Canyon–Woodrow Canyon Trail provides excellent
access between Mogollon Creek on the north and Turkey Creek on
the south. The climb on both sides is rugged and steep, but well
worth it—the view from the 8,000-foot ridge in between them is
spectacular. It takes about two and a half to three hours to complete
the trail (twice what it would take to cover the same linear distance in
the flat country). Vegetation is similar to that found elsewhere in the
Gila: south-facing slopes are predominantely covered with piñon-
juniper, and north-facing slopes are vegetated with ponderosa pine.
Woodrow Canyon is narrow in places, more so than Sycamore Canyon. This trail sees little use and in places may be obstructed by
deadfall. Fishing in both Mogollon Creek on the north and Turkey
Creek on the south can be good at times. Water is normally found in
both Sycamore and Woodrow canyons year-round. Woodrow will be
intermittent to dry in the dry season.

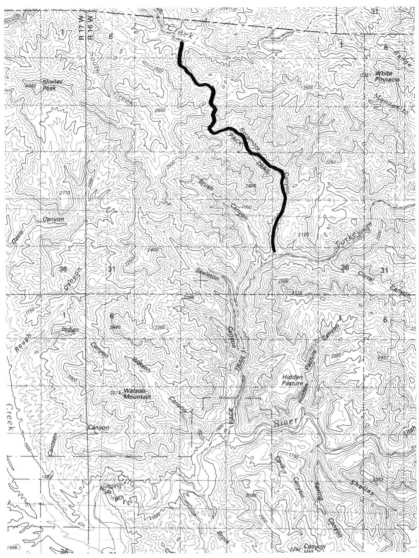

Sycamore Canyon–Woodrow Canyon Trail

Contour interval 50 meters

Wild grape vines cascade off an oak branch along Turkey Creek near Sycamore Canyon. (Photograph by John Murray)

*74 Mountain–Mogollon Creek Trail** (U.S.F.S. #153)

Trailhead elevation (near Rice Ranch): 5,300 feet
Trail ending (Woodrow Canyon): 7,040 feet
Total vertical ascent: 1,740 feet
Length: 13.50 miles (21.60 kilometers)
Recommended season: April through November, except in
    periods of high water (spring runoff or flash floods)
Use: Moderate to heavy (especially during hunting seasons)
Difficulty: Moderate
U.S.G.S. maps: Shelley Peak

Access: Drive west of Silver City on U.S. 180 past,
consecutively, Mangas Valley, Mangas Springs, and
Greenwood Canyon. Turn right or north on State Highway
293 at Cliff. At mile 3.5 turn left or northwest on Forest Route
147. Drive north about ten miles. Turn right at the sign, "L.
Shelley 916 Ranch." Road ends at Rice Ranch Trailhead.
Because the trailhead is located very near private land, the
following rules need to be observed. Persons are requested to
park vehicles 100 yards east of the trailhead and not near stock
water. Also, do not use private facilities or trespass unless
permission is obtained, preferably in writing, from the
owners.

  *The 74 Mountain–Mogollon Creek Trails in the Silver City District for the
first seven miles and in the Wilderness District for the last six and one half
miles.

The 74 Mountain–Mogollon Creek Trail provides access to 74
Mountain, Bud's Hole, and the headwaters of Mogollon Creek. The
trailhead is very popular during hunting seasons, both archery and
rifle, for deer and elk. Also for backpackers this route may be easier
than many to reach adjoining areas in the Gila Wilderness. Fishing for
trout on Mogollon Creek can be quite good at certain times of the

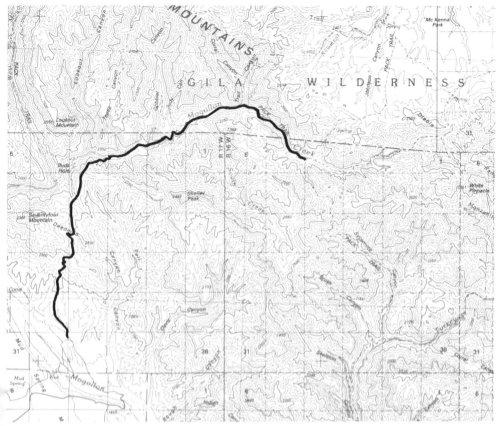

74 MOUNTAIN-MOGOLLON CREEK TRAIL   Contour interval 50 meters

year. Water availability is a problem along the trail until it reaches Mogollon Creek. During the wet season, water may be sometimes found in Deadman Canyon, but this source is not reliable. Once Mogollon Creek is reached, clear water is no problem

A distance of 5.50 miles is covered from the trailhead to the junction with Trail #189 (see the Rain Creek–Bud's Hole Trail description). Most of this distance is exposed with little or no shade. It can be quite uncomfortable during the hot months of the year. From the junction with Trail #189, it is a distance of 1.25 miles down into

Bud's Hole on #189, and then 2.00 miles to Mogollon Creek on #153. Trail #221, up Gobbler Canyon to Snow Park high in the Mogollon Creek on #153. Trail #221, up Gobbler Canyon to Snow Park high in the Mogollon Mountains, appears on the left at mile 9.5. 74 Mountain–Mogollon Creek Trail formally turns away from Mogollon Creek at Trail Canyon, two miles east of Gobbler Canyon, but most hikers continue on into the headwaters of the Creek. At mile 13.5 Woodrow Canyon appears on the right or south (see Woodrow Canyon–Sycamore Canyon Trail description). Hiking beyond this point on Trail #153 leads to Turnbo Canyon, McKenna Park, and, eventually, Little Creek Spring at the headwaters of Turkey Creek. After leaving Mogollon Creek, Trail #153 heads east towards Mc-Kenna Park. This trail, starting from 74 Mountain, offers some excellent camping locations and fishing opportunities for the backcountry traveler. Most would consider this an easy-to-moderate hike.

Rain Creek–Bud's Hole Trail (U.S.F.S. #189)

Trailhead elevation (Rain Creek Mesa): 6,050 feet
Trail ending (Mogollon Creek): 6,100 feet
Total vertical ascent (high point of 7,000 feet): 950 feet
Length: 8.25 miles (13.20 kilometers)
Recommended season: April through November
Use: Light
Difficulty: Difficult
U.S.G.S. maps: Rice Ranch, Shelley Peak

Access: Proceed west of Silver City on U.S. 180 past, consecutively, Cliff, Buckthorn, and Leopold Vista Historical Monument. One mile north of the monument, and just before Soldier Hill, turn right or east on Forest Service Road 147. Drive approximately ten miles east, over Little Dry Creek and Sacaton Creek to Rain Creek Mesa. Main trail begins above Rain Creek, adjacent to Forest Road 147. Vehicles should park near road signed as "Sacaton Trailhead" and not on private land nearby. As with all parts of the Gila country, backcountry users should respect the rights of landowners.

In comparison with many other Wilderness trails described in this book, the area of Rain Creek and Bud's Hole penetrated by U.S.F.S. #189 sees relatively light use and is very scenic and rugged. Exceptional views exist between Rain Creek and the West Fork of Mogollon Creek. Lookout Mountain (8,425 feet), used by Geronimo and his warriors to watch avenues of approach to their sanctuaries in the area (particularly at the headwaters of Tepee Canyon), can be seen a short distance to the north and east. To the south, the mesa country leading into Old Mexico can be seen. In places, the trail is very steep and difficult. Water is scarce between the creeks, and hikers are advised to carry their own water supplies over the trail.

It is a distance of one mile from the trailhead to Rain Creek, and then five miles from Rain Creek to the West Fork of Mogollon Creek.

The enormous white blossom of a buffalo gourd plant in Rain Creek.
(Photograph by Charles William Murray, Junior)

From this point it is 2.25 miles to Bud's Hole on Mogollon Creek.
Parts of the trail are extremely steep and difficult and may be inadvis-
able for some saddle and packstock. These areas include the climb
from Rain Creek, the half-mile west of the West Fork of Mogollon
Creek, and the climb out of the West Fork where bedrock is exposed
on the trail surface for approximately 100 yards. Those on foot should
not have the problems that steel-shod horses and mules do in these
sections. Water is found only on Rain Creek, the West Fork of Mogo-

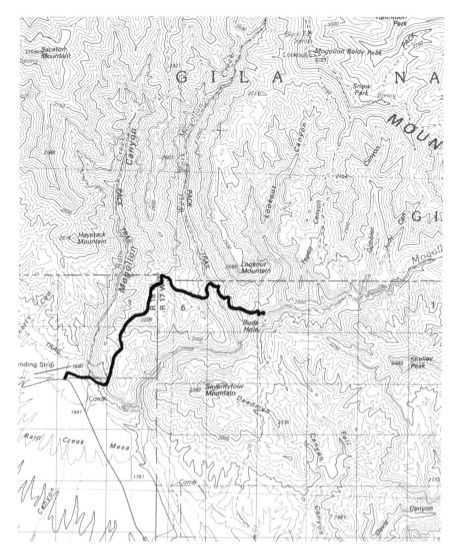

RAIN CREEK–BUD'S HOLE TRAIL   Contour interval 50 meters

llon Creek, and Mogollon Creek. There is no water to be found in between these drainages.

Important spur trails located along the Rain Creek–Bud's Hole Trail are as follows, with mileages from the trailhead: Rain Creek Trail (undeveloped—0.50 miles), West Fork of Mogollon Creek Trail #224 (5.50 miles), and 74 Mountain or Rice Ranch Trail #153 (1.00 miles past Mogollon Creek, 9.25 miles from trailhead).

David Brown, in his book *The Grizzly in the Southwest* (see "Further Reading"), reports that the last grizzly bear in New Mexico was killed on Rain Creek in the spring of 1931. The April 17, 1931, edition of the *Silver City Enterprise* contains the following report:

To Carl and Blue Rice of Cliff goes the credit for killing one of the largest grizzly bears ever seen in this section. They were riding their range and came upon a dead cow on Rain Creek, and finding the tracks of a big grizzly bear around the carcass, they went to the nearest phone and called up Supervisor James A. Scott and asked him to secure from the state game department a special permit for killing the bear out of season.

Just over the border, in neighboring Arizona, the last grizzly bear in that state was killed in Stray Horse Canyon, northeast of Clifton, by Richard Miller, a PARC hunter (Predator and Rodent Control Department of the U.S. Biological Survey) on September 13, 1935. The year 1935 was a drought year and because of the scarcity of their natural foods, these bears, largely vegetarians, turned at times to livestock. This area is today protected by the Blue Range Primitive Area. In 1936 the Forest Service began to consider measures to protect the great bears, but is was too late. They were all gone.

TURKEY CREEK TRAIL (U.S.F.S. #155)

Trailhead elevation (confluence with Gila River): 4,770 feet
Trail ending (Little Creek Spring): 7,300 feet
Total vertical ascent (high point of 7,900 feet): 3,130 feet
Length: 19.25 miles (30.80 kilometers)
Recommended season: April through November, except in
  periods of high water (spring runoff or flash floods)
Use: Moderate
Difficulty: Moderate to difficult
U.S.G.S. maps: Diablo Range, Little Turkey Park, Canyon
  Hill, Canteen Canyon

Access: Drive west of Silver City on U.S. 180 past,
consecutively, Mangas Valley, Mangas Springs, and
Greenwood Canyon. Turn right or north on State Highway
211 and drive through Gila (the road becomes State Highway
293 north of town). At the national forest boundary, 4.5 miles
from Gila, the road becomes a four-wheel drive road. Take
this road, National Forest Road 155, down Brushy Canyon to
the Gila River and to the Turkey Creek Trailhead, located
across the river at the confluence of Turkey Creek and the Gila
River. Near the trailhead is a small portion of private land
with buildings. Please respect the rights of these landowners.

The Turkey Creek Trail follows Turkey Creek throughout its entire
length in the Gila Wilderness, from its confluence with the Gila River
to its headwaters near Granite Peak (8,731 feet). Unlike many trails in
the region, water is plentiful along the trail, as it remains close to the
stream through most of its duration. From the trailhead at the Gila
River, the trail follows the creek bottom to Skeleton Canyon (mile
2.50), where it leaves the bottom for approximately 2.75 miles. The
climb and ridge trail from Skeleton to Sycamore Canyon (mile 5.25)
is on a south-exposed mountainside, which can be extremely hot
during the summer months. Horse travel in this area, combined with

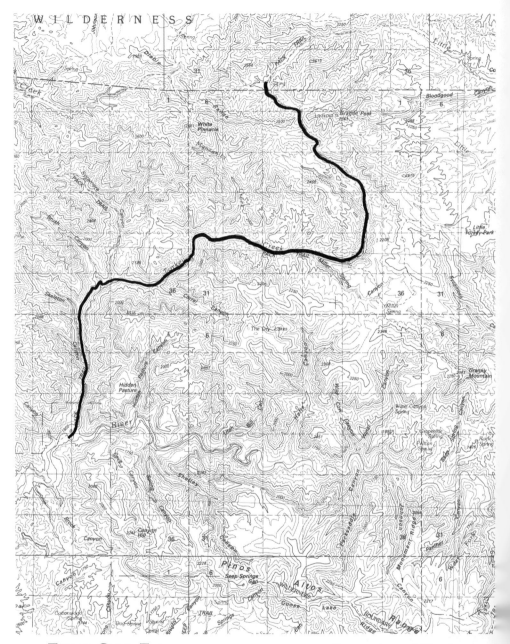

TURKEY CREEK TRAIL   Contour interval 50 meters

many creek crossings, is fairly difficult. The Sycamore Canyon–Woodrow Canyon Trail #158 is located at the mouth of Sycamore Canyon (mile 5.25). The Miller Spring Trail #159 is to the south or right at mile 13.25. During dry months, Turkey Creek becomes intermittent above the confluence with Miller Spring Canyon. The spur trail to Granite Creek (U.S.F.S. #150) is on the right or east at mile 18.00. The Little Creek Trail (U.S.F.S. #161) is reached at mile 19.25, and the Little Creek Spring, located at the juncture, runs clear water year-round. Trail #155 actually runs farther on beyond this point, traversing McKenna Park and then descending White Creek to the Middle Fork.

By far the most popular hike on Turkey Creek is to the hot springs, located about 4.0 miles from the trailhead on the Gila River, and about 1.5 miles from the point the trail cuts up Skeleton Ridge and rims over to Sycamore Canyon. There is no maintained trail to the hot springs. Extensive wading and bouldering is necessary to reach it. The springs are not accessible to horses. Despite these obstacles, the area receives high use and hikers should be environmentally conscious when using the springs. Pack out everything you pack in.

Henry Woodrow, the first ranger in the Gila Country, writes in his memoirs that the last of the Apaches lived in this area:

The only time I ever saw wild Indians was in 1900. There used to be a renegade Apache Indian who lived in the mountains with a squaw and two or three children. . . . Part of the time he made his headquarters in the Mogollon Mountains at the head of Mogollon Creek and of Turkey Creek. . . . On this trip in 1900 Horn Silver Bill and I got up in a rough side canyon at the head of Mogollon Creek [near the headwaters of Turkey Creek] and ran onto these Indians. They saw us and started running off behind some big rocks. We turned our horses and ran the other way, back to where there were some other people camped on Turkey Creek. This was the last and only time I ever saw the Indians, although I saw their tracks several times after that. The Chief was finally killed in the north end of the Black Range, and the squaw returned to San Carlos Indian Reservation.

Today not one of the original Chiricahua Apache inhabit their former homelands in the Gila Country or in the Chiricahua Mountains over

Fresh bear scat, showing recently eaten acorns, on the Turkey Creek Trail. Knife is five inches long. (Photograph by John Murray)

the border in southeastern Arizona. The tribe lives in Oklahoma and elsewhere in New Mexico (Mescalero Reservation). As late as 1979, the grandchildren of Geronimo and Cochise still lived on these reservations.

During spring runoff periods or other high water times, backpackers will want to take a pair of tennis shoes for the frequent stream crossings that must be made. A familiar bird to travelers on the Turkey Creek Trail is the dipper or water ouzel (*Cinclus mexicanus*), which lives in and around streams throughout the West. The ouzel, a slate gray, wren-shaped bird with a stubby tail and yellowish feet, will often be seen diving into the water from its rocky perches. It runs along the bottom in shallow areas with half-opened wings, picking among the gravel, debris, and sand for morsels of food. Suddenly it will explode from the water and return to its perch, nibbling on a larvae or a nymph. The ouzels are vigorous singers, their loud bubbling song often carrying over the noise of rapids and waterfalls. In the spring the ouzels build their nests among the roots and rocks of bank side areas, lining them with moss and leaves. In the winter, the bird prefers to remain on its home stream, but will migrate to lower areas if the weather becomes too severe for it. Its cheerful song is always welcome to hikers weary from the trail and often a good excuse to sit down and take a rest while watching this amusing little fellow make his livelihood on the stream.

SPRING CANYON TRAIL* (U.S.F.S. #247)

Trailhead elevation (Sapillo Creek): 5,950 feet
Trail ending (Gila River): 5,100 feet
Total vertical ascent: 850 feet
Length: 6.50 miles (10.40 kilometers)
Recommended season: April through November
Use: Moderate
Difficulty: Moderate
U.S.G.S. maps: Copperas Peak, Granny Mountain

Access: Drive north from Silver City on New Mexico 15 past, consecutively, Pinos Altos, the Ben Lilly Memorial Marker, Cherry Creek Campground, McMillan Campground, and Lookout Point. At mile 26.2 is the junction with New Mexico 35 to Lake Roberts and San Lorenzo. The main trail begins approximately 0.25 miles west of State Highway 15 (just before the junction with New Mexico 35) on Sapillo Creek.

*The Spring Canyon Trail is actually in the Silver City District, but is included here because it leads into the Wilderness.

The Spring Canyon Trail, like the Packsaddle Canyon Trail (U.S.F.S. #732) farther to the west, provides convenient access to the Gila River within the Wilderness primarily for fishermen, but also for deer hunters as well. The advantage of this trail over that in Packsaddle Canyon is that the trailhead can be reached by two-wheel drive vehicles. Goose Lake, from which the Packsaddle Canyon Trail begins, is accessible only to those on foot, horseback, or with a four-wheel drive vehicle. The Spring Canyon Trailhead is only a short distance from a major paved highway.

The trail climbs to the north of Sapillo Creek and parallels it until it drops back into the canyon approximately 0.5 miles from the Gila River. Most of the length of the trail traverses south-facing hillsides

SPRING CANYON TRAIL   Contour interval 50 meters

with limited shade, which makes hiking uncomfortably hot during
the summer months. This same disadvantage makes the trail an attractive route during the cooler months of the year. Water is found on
Sapillo Creek at the trailhead, then again when the trail returns to the
canyon bottom, and of course at the confluence with the Gila River.
Wet springs can be sometimes found on canyon bottoms along the
trail. At the point where the trail drops back towards Sapillo Creek,
approximately 0.5 miles from the Gila River, it is quite rocky and

steep for about 100 yards, and it is recommended that saddle and packstock be led through this section.

A popular route during the autumn and spring, the Spring Canyon Trail offers some spectacular views of the Sapillo Box. It should be noted that if hikers remain in the creek bottom while en route to the river, they will be faced with extensive wading and rock climbing. This route can be impassable during high water periods and in the flash flood season. Stock cannot be taken into the creek bottom. Finally, cattle may be encountered throughout the Spring Canyon Trail, and all gates should be left as secure as they are found.

EPILOGUE

Amidst the downward tendency and proneness of things, when every voice is raised for a new road or another statute . . . will you not tolerate one or two solitary voices in the land, speaking for thoughts and principles not marketable or perishable?

> —Ralph Waldo Emerson, *The Transcendentalist* (a lecture read in the Masonic Temple, Boston, January 1842)

A Perfect Day in the Gila

"One day contains the whole of my life."
—Martial

A perfect day in the Gila country begins early. In the wilderness I never sleep late, for there is much to do and much to be missed. Back in the city I may sleep for several hours into the day. Sometimes in the winter the sun has cleared the trees at the end of the street and melted the snow from the newspaper and I am still sound asleep. But that is in the city. In the mountains I am always anxious to be up with the first birds, or before, in order to squeeze the most from each day. When I was younger and carried a rod or rifle, the reason for an early start was simple: I wished to get my game. Now that I am older, though, and have outgrown what Thoreau called the "embryo" or "hunter stage of development," the prey I seek can be brought back home in the creel or game bag of my mind: insights, images, inspirations, ideas, and observations. As Thoreau stipulated, there comes a time when a person leaves "the hunter and fisher" behind and re-enters nature "as a poet and naturalist . . . the gun and fish-pole behind."

In the cold black hours before dawn, stretched out in my sleeping bag on the sand beside the West Fork of the Gila River, I am the sole owner of the canyon. No one is up yet. The land is quiet, still, resting. The plants and trees are in repose; the molecular miracle of chlorophyll is inactive. The animals are, to be sure, up and about. There is some rustling over in a patch of prickly pear cactus; probably a racoon or striped skunk eating the ripe red fruit. From the top of a towering ponderosa an owl hoots resonately, no doubt sending the field mice scurrying for their burrows near the well-armored yuccas. Though I can't see them, the bats are about. Soon they will be returning to caves in the cliffs, their furry little bellies fat with mosquitoes and moths. In the evergreen woodlands above camp the black bears are eating the acorns and juniper berries. Even the gray fox, known as the "tree fox" for its arboreal habits, is climbing through the branches harvesting the early fall nuts. The mule deer are getting up stiffly from their beds in the deep pine needles beneath the pinyons. Soon they will be moving down the slopes toward water. Somewhere a mountain lion is climbing among the volcanic pinnacles near a place where the javelinas might pass in the morning. There is a whole night life to the wilderness. A book could be written just on the natural history of the night in the desert uplands.

Below camp the river murmurs quietly over the smooth rounded stones in its channel. Listening to the river reminds me of the time I put on a stethescope and listened to the systole and diastole of a human heart. The rivers are the arteries of the desert wilderness: big, fat, pulsing with green life. Without them, the wilderness as we know it would cease to exist. The rocks would still be there, the barren ridge lines protruding like the bones of a skeleton, but there would be no flesh on them; few if any plants and little or no animal life. Water is the life blood in the desert as it is in few other ecosystems. An inch here or an inch there can make the difference between fruit and seed, drought and disaster. Over the rocks of a riffle and down the falls into a pool, the river plays a soft, relaxing harmony like a three-noted minor chord alternating seamlessly with a major chord. It begins to lull me back to sleep, but I resist, because I want to watch the day begin, second by eternal second, as it did before me and as it will long after me.

Orion, the first of the winter constellations, is rising in the east. Behind it is Sirius, the dog star of the Egyptians, a star that foretold the coming of the harvest each year. A blue meteor suddenly streaks across the western sky with the brilliance of a signal flare, and then, as if smashing into an invisible wall, it explodes brightly, the long dying streamers trailing off silently through the stars. I wait for another, but none comes. Some scientists believe that meteors brought the essential ingredients of life—the complex hydrocarbon molecules—into the petri dish environment of primitive Earth over three billion years ago.

At 4:47 a.m. the first bird calls out, a whip-poor-will: prrrrip-pooor-rilll! Called by the locals the night jar, he repeats his song tirelessly, a cheerful rolling melody that soon awakens other birds. At 5:14 a.m. a lazuli bunting joins in: sweet-sweet chew-chew seet chew. Ten minutes later I hear a solitary vireo in a willow thicket: chuwee, cheereo, bzurrp, chuweer, a loud rich song. Fifteen minutes pass and the sky to the east begins to lighten. The owl is long gone by now and the whip-poor-will is silent. The day birds begin to awaken: the ubiquitous American robin with his song recalling "cheer-up, cheer-ily!," the black-capped chicadee with his song like his name "chi-cadee-dee-deee," and a yellow warbler singing "sweet-sweet-sweet-sweet-setta se-see-whew!" No chorus of the Vienna choir or the Mormon Tabernacle choir ever sounded so magnificently. By 6:00 I hear the first turkey gobble in the cliffs above the river. A woodpecker pounds a ponderosa. A hummingbird buzzes by as the sky rapidly brightens. A pair of ravens launch their first patrol of the canyon, cawwing down into the immense gulf below them, an abyss in which I must seem an insignificant speck. Far to the east a scaffolding of clouds as thin as the timbers on Cavalry ignites and burns red for a moment. The day has begun.

With the first camp robber pecking over last night's dinner my father is up and quickly starting a fire, the bacon sizzling in the pan, the eggs broken in and turning white in the heat. I tell him my plan for the morning, to hike to the Meadows, a lovely place eight miles distant on the Middle Fork of the Gila. He would prefer that I stay, but knows I am determined to make the hike. His favorite quotation is from Ghandi: "Wherever you are, be there." He knows I want to make the most of my stay. I quickly fill my pack with "liquids and edibles," and set off down the trail.

I turn at the first bend.

"I'll meet you at TJ corral at 1:00. We'll go horseback riding then."

He smiles and waves, already shooting photographs of ancient Mogollon petroglyphs on the canyon wall. Painted red with a hematite compound, the paintings have endured the ages and shine brightly in the first light of the day. Some are formed in vivid patterns and geometric designs. Others present the familiar human figure, forever waving across the abyss of time.

In a very short time I am several miles back in the Gila Wilderness, a place that will never know a seismic test hole, a whining power saw, a surveyor's transit, a lumbering earth-mover, a concrete mixer's roar, or the sad dreary sound of a radio or a television. It will be up there for all time, free and wild, sprawling with solitude and beauty, a realm immune to the county clerk's record books and the Probate court's division of ancestral estates. Thanks to the vision and vigor of Aldo Leopold, each generation will be able to explore this *terra incognita*, this "blank place on the map," and return to civilization renewed and relaxed. Because it is so large, the Gila is a horseman's country. The West Fork and Middle Fork trails go upwards of forty miles, and some of the longer loop trails push close to one hundred miles. A good mountain horse and a sturdy pack mule are indispensable. So is a faithful hound. For many years the backcountry, that is to say the true

An enormous old grey oak along the West Fork of the Gila River. (Photograph by John Murray)

outback, places like the blown-down timber on Mogollon Baldy or the grassy meadows of McKenna Park, were the sole domain of the mounted rider, but since World War II innovations in backpacking gear have opened these regions to a person on foot. Today a person on foot can go anywhere in the wilderness, including places were a horse or mule can't travel. Backpackers now penetrate as far and stay as long as horsepackers. Some people want to eliminate horses and mules from the Gila, but I don't have any problem with horses in the wilderness so long as they're managed properly. In fact, its nice to know they're around in a pinch. Closing the wilderness cabins, on the other hand, was probably a good idea.

Crossing the West Fork in a wide place below the Zig Zag trail, I startle a Great Blue Heron, who utters a loud, raucous "grak, grak, grak," as he slowly brings himself up from the water. He flaps heavily overhead on tremendous blue-gray wings, his long neck folded back slightly on the shoulder as he stares over at me. I can see the black pupils flashing indignantly in his wide yellow eyes. The herons are protected a few miles downstream by the Heart Bar Wildlife Refuge. Fishing is good for the big birds on the West Fork. A few days earlier, my father and I counted twenty trout in one deep pool beneath a canyon wall.

Some miles later, stone-hopping the small spring-fed stream at the head of Big Bear Canyon, I hear a young elk bugle nearby. It is a high-pitched whistle, just testing the voice as the first hormones stir, and ends more in a shriek than in a grunt. There is elk scat on the trail, some of it warm to the touch, and I pass a camp of bow-hunters near the stream. They are sitting around the camp-fire, staring at the flames. They do not hear me pass. If they heard the elk they do not show it. Tomorrow is opening day. Once the Merriam's elk made its home in the Gila, but it was hunted into extinction earlier in the century. Now the Yellowstone elk, imported from Wyoming, roams the uplands. Many other species were hunted into extinction at this time: the gray wolf, the grizzly bear, the river otter, the bighorn sheep, the jaguar. Only the bighorn sheep has been brought back, but there are many, including me, who believe that all of the species, certainly the otter and grizzly, could be easily restored to the Gila country. Leaving the little stream I recall some lines from the poet Thomas Hardy:

> The purl of a runlet that never ceases
> In stir of kingdoms, in wars, in peaces;
> With a hollow boiling voice it speaks
> And has spoken since hills were turfless peaks.

On the final approach to the rim of the canyon above the Middle Fork, the open, parklike ponderosa forest is quiet and still, almost solemn. Through the trees I see a light coming up from the depths of the Earth. It is the reflected light of the canyon, here over one thousand feet deep. I walk slowly, consciously retarding my step as my anticipation grows. Finally I stand at the edge of the great gulf, the immense ponderosas below as small as from a plane, the roar of the river a distant whisper. "Cluck, Cluck, Cluck." I look up and a silver-tailed Abert's squirrel is talking to me. These squirrels live only in ponderosa forests, where they feed on the twigs and cones. "How fearful/And dizzy 'tis to cast one's eyes so low!" said Edgar in *King Lear* as he and Gloucester stood on the Dover Cliffs, but I feel none of that vertigo now and gaze into the vastness, marveling at the power of an element as insubstantial as water to create such a chasm. There are those who would like to dam the Gila River near its mouth, but I am not one of them. The Gila is one of the last free-flowing rivers in the Southwest, and I hope it stays that way.

My father and I arrive at Doc Campbell's corral shortly after one. Dad has spent the morning photographing the Gila Cliff Dwellings and talking with the interpretive ranger, Everett Whitehead, a fifth generation resident of southwestern New Mexico. Becky Campbell, one of Doc's children, is at the corral to greet us. Becky is surrounded by a bevy of seven or eight of the finest-looking lion and bear hounds I've ever seen. One of them, she tells me, is descended from the hunting stock of the famous hunter Ben Lilly. She takes us over to a large outdoor freezer and pulls out the skull and pelt of a freshly-killed black bear, taken the day before in Little Turkey Park after a short chase. The fur of the bear is long, smooth, and jet black. He was a big bear, weighing close to three hundred pounds, and his huge front paws dwarf my hands as I examine them. Becky explains that she had treed a bear the week before but, seeing it was a female with cubs from the condition of the mammaries, didn't kill it. Becky is a good hunter. She invites me along to observe a lion hunt in January and I accept. "It will be good for you as a writer," she says, and I readily agree.

One of the hounds, a half-crippled old redbone named Ranger, leads us out of the corral and down through the cottonwoods and alders to the river. His nose and head are deeply scarred from the teeth and claws of lions and bears, but even at the venerable age of thirteen he is still eager to wander down the river into the wilderness with us. Over my back I tell my father the story of the homecoming of Odysseus. Returning from ten year's of wandering after the Trojan War, the great warrior entered Ithaca disguised as a beggar so that he could observe the state of his kingdom. Despite the disguise, his

The black-tailed rattlesnake waited on the side of the trail for us to leave. Notice the extraordinary camoflage of this reptile, with the black tail in the lower right. (Photograph by John Murray)

faithful old hound Argos recognizes Odysseus and wags his tail for him one last time before he dies:

> When Argos heard
> Odysseus' voice nearby he did his best
> To wag his tail, nose down, with flattened ears,
> having no strength to move nearer his master.
> And Odysseus looked away,
> wiping a salt tear from his cheek; but he
> hid this from Eumaios . . . for death and darkness
> in that instant closed
> the eyes of old Argos, who had seen his master,
> Odysseus, after twenty years.

Returning up the Gila Ranger turns and barks a warning. Just ahead a black-tailed rattlesnake is curled and buzzing in the middle of the trail. My father and I dismount from our horses Pearl and Judd and walk them through the trees around the trail. When we are on the other side we tie the horses off and return to shoot pictures of the snake, a beautiful green serpent with irregular blotches along the length of its back. The last three inches of tail are a dark black. We count six rattles at the end of the tail. He is fat and sluggish and makes no effort to strike or retreat, but if we attempt to get closer than eight feet he begins to rattle. We turn to leave and after a few steps I turn and look back. He is already gone.

After putting the horses back in the corral we drive up the road to Woody's Corral where we have a fire-cooked dinner of beef stew, biscuits, and beer. Sitting on the stump of a recently cut ponderosa, I begin to count the annual rings. Twenty-one inches from the center I find my last one: three hundred and fourteen, meaning that the tree first began growing in 1673 or thereabouts. My father and I reflect on the profound changes that have occurred on the American continent in the last three centuries, the Anglo culture pushing inexorably from the first strongholds in New England and the Middle Atlantic states while the Hispanic culture expanded north into Colorado, west into California, and east into Texas. Just a few hours from this tree the first atomic bomb was exploded in 1945 and a little to the south there is now a spaceport at White Sands where the space shuttle could land in a pinch. And yet, despite all these changes, my father and I can still sit and watch the cliff swallows swerve and dart over the last hatch of the day, as Geronimo did during the 1840s when he was a boy growing up on the West Fork of the Gila. We both agree the true test of a civilization is in its ability to preserve wilderness values while at the same time expanding its base of science and technology to the stars.

The last event of the day is a quiet visit to the home of Doc and Ida Campbell, who earlier invited us over for tea and coffee around seven. Doc came to the Gila country from the East in 1930. His first job was as a mule packer. Ida is the great step-daughter of Thomas Lyons, who built the Lyons hunting lodge where Theodore Roosevelt "almost came to hunt one year." Doc tells my father and I stories about Ben Lilly, who was seventy-five years old when he met him, and Nat Straw, another hunter who made his camp near the confluence of Little Creek and the Gila River. Ben Lilly referred to Nat Straw as "that old gentlemen Mr. Straw" and Nat Straw in similar politeness always inquired about the status of "Mr. Lilly." Doc relates that, curiously, the two famous hunters who lived within a day's ride of one another never met. Nat Straw had an octagon-barrelled .32 Winchester special rifle with which he killed ninety-three bears. Doc's funniest story concerns two men from Chicago he took turkey hunting. After placing them behind blinds near a stock pond, he heard shooting and quickly returned. The men had killed a black bear. The three of them field-dressed the animal and, to protect it from coyotes, hung the carcass over a cliff with a rope. When they returned with a packhorse the next morning, the bear was frozen solid. The only way the bear could be packed out was sitting upright in the saddle. Still frozen upon returning to the valley, they left the bear in the ranch shower and got alot of laughs watching the cowboys react when they saw the bear.

Hours later, pleading exhaustion, we finally leave the warm hospitality of the Campbell's and return to Woody's Corral where we will camp for the night. Not bothering to restart the fire, we pull out our sleeping bags and climb inside. As I lay there falling sleeping, I think about another father and son, Sylvester Pattie and James Ohio Pattie, who camped not one mile from us on January 25, 1825. They, too, were originally from Ohio, and they also came into the Gila country when it was a wilderness. The next day Sylvester and James split up, James ascending the Middle Fork and Sylvester exploring the West Fork. It was on the Middle Fork that James killed a grizzly bear so large "that we extracted ten gallons of oil from it." A few days later they found an American the Apaches had killed. The mountains were dangerous then, when the first beaver trappers came west on the Santa Fe Trail.

"John. John. John."

My father calls to me in a whisper.

"What?"

"Listen."

A mountain lion is screaming from the rocks behind our camp, as eerie a sound as was ever made by any animal on earth.

After awhile the lion tires of his sport and vanishes into the night. It

Happy Trails! Pictured is Ysabel Campbell leading a packtrain across Snow Park deep in the Gila Wilderness. (Photograph with permission by Doc Campbell)

has been a good, long, hard day. I think of the quotation in the scripture from St. John (9:4): "That night cometh when no man can work," a line that Samuel Johnson was fond of quoting. I have made good use of the day. It has been as full as I could make it. The frogs are chanting in the grass and luring me off to sleep. Before I can finish the next thought I am asleep.

Further Reading

There are men who love out-of-doors who yet never open a book; and other men who love books but to whom the great book of nature is a sealed volume, and the lines written therein blurred and illegible. Nevertheless among those men whom I have known the love of books and the love of outdoors, in their highest expressions, have usually gone hand in hand. Usually the keenest appreciation of what is seen in nature is to be found in those who have also profited by the hoarded and recorded wisdom of their fellow men. Love of outdoor life, love of simple and hardy pastimes, can be gratified by men and women who do not possess large means, and who work hard; and so can love of books. . . .
—Theodore Roosevelt, *Autobiography* (1913)

I. ANIMALS

Brown, David E. 1985. *The Grizzly in the Southwest*. Norman: University of Oklahoma Press.

————. 1983. *The Wolf in the Southwest*. Tucson: University of Arizona Press.

Dodge, N.N. 1968. *Poisonous Dwellers of the Desert*. Globe, Ariz.: Southwest Parks and Monuments Association.

Murie, Olaus. 1954. *Field Guide to Animal Tracks*. Boston: Houghton Mifflin Co.

O'Connor, Jack. 1967. *Big Game Hunting in North America*. New York: Knopf.

Olin, G., and E. Bierly. 1961. *Mammals of the Southwest Mountains and Mesas*. Globe: Southwest Parks and Monuments Association.

Olin, G., and J. Cannon. 1965. *Mammals of the Southwest Deserts*. Globe: Southwest Parks and Monuments Association.

Udvardy, Miklos. 1977. *The Audubon Field Guide to North American Birds* (Western Region). New York: Knopf.

II. ARCHAEOLOGY

Giammettei, V.M., and N.G. Reichert. 1975. *Art of a Vanishing Race*. Woodland, Calif.: Dillon-Tyler.

Martin, P.S., G.I. Quimby, and D. Collier. 1947. *Indians before Columbus*. Chicago: University of Chicago Press.

Wheat, J.B. 1955. *Mogollon Culture prior to* A.D. *1000*. American Anthropological Association, Mem. 82.

III. FOSSILS

Clark, D.L. 1968. *Fossils, Paleontology, and Evolution*. Dubuque, Iowa: Wm. C. Brown.

Cowen, R. 1976. *History of Life*. New York: McGraw-Hill.

Fenton, C.L., and M.A. Fenton. 1958. *The Fossil Book*. New York: Doubleday.

Laporte, L.F. 1968. *Ancient Environments*. Englewood Cliffs, N.J.: Prentice Hall.

Matthews, W.H. 1962. *Fossils, An Introduction to Prehistoric Life*. New York: Barnes and Noble.

McAlester, A.L. 1968. *The History of Life*. Englewood Cliffs, N.J.: Prentice Hall.

Ratkevich, R., and N. LaFon. 1978. *Field Guide to New Mexico Fossils*. Alamogordo, N. Mex.: Dinograph Southwest.

Rhodes, F.H., H.S. Zim, and P.R. Shaffer. 1962. *Fossils*. New York: Colden Press.

Shimer, H.W., and R.R. Schrock. 1944. *Index Fossils of North America*. New York: John Wiley.

IV. GENERAL

Abbey, Edward. 1968. *Desert Solitaire, A Season in the Wilderness*. New York: Random House.

———. 1977. *The Journey Home, Some Words in the Defense of the American West*. New York: Dutton.

———. 1982. *Down the River*. New York: Dutton.

———. 1983. *Beyond the Wall*. New York: Holt, Rinehart, and Winston.

Back, Joe. 1959. *Horses, Hitches, and Rocky Trails*. Chicago: Sage Books.

Bergon, Frank (ed.). 1980. *The Wilderness Reader*. New York: Mentor.

Brooks, Paul. 1980. *Speaking For Nature, How Literary Naturalists from Henry Thoreau to Rachel Carson Have Shaped America*. San Francisco: Sierra Club.

Jones, F. 1968. *Old Mines and Ghost Camps of New Mexico*. Reprinted from New Mexico Mines and Minerals, 1905. Fort Davis, Tex.: Frontier Book Co.

Kesler, S.E. 1976. *Our Finite Mineral Resources*. New York: McGraw-Hill.

Krauskopf, K.B. 1974. *The Third Planet, An Invitation to Geology*. San Francisco: Freeman Cooper.

Leopold, Aldo. 1976. *A Sand County Almanac, With Essays on Conservation from Round River*. Reprinted with permission of Oxford University Press. New York: Ballantine.

McFarland, E.F. 1967. *Forever Frontier, the Gila Cliff Dwellings*. Albuquerque: University of New Mexico Press.

Oppelt, Norman. 1981. *Guide to Prehistoric Ruins of the Southwest*. Boulder, Colo.: Pruett.

Pearce, T. M. 1965. *New Mexico Place Names*. Albuquerque: University of New Mexico Press.

Schullery, Paul. 1984. *Mountain Time*. New York: Nick Lyons Books.

Schultheis, Bob. 1983. *The Hidden West, Journeys in the American Outback*. San Francisco: North Point Press.

Sutton, Ann, and Myron Sutton. 1974. *Wilderness Areas of North America*. New York: Funk and Wagnalls.

Tejada-Flores, Lito. 1978. *Wildwater, The Sierra Club Guide to Kayaking and Whitewater Boating*. San Francisco: Sierra Club Books.

Ungnade, H.E. 1972. *Guide to the New Mexico Mountains*. 2d ed. Albuquerque: University of New Mexico Press.

Wallace, David Rains. 1983. *The Klamath Knot*. San Francisco: Sierra Club Books.

Zwinger, Ann. 1978. *Beyond the Aspen Grove*. New York: Harper and Row.

v. GEOLOGY

Armstrong, A. K. 1962. *Stratigraphy and Paleontology of the Mississippian System in Southwestern New Mexico and Adjacent Southeastern Arizona*. New Mexico Bureau of Mines and Mineral Resources, Mem. 8.

Clemons, Russell E., Paige W. Christiansen, and H.L. James. 1980. *Southwestern New Mexico, Scenic Trips to the Geologic Past*. No. 10, revised. Socorro: New Mexico Bureau of Mines and Mineral Resources.

vi. HISTORY

Christiansen, P.W. 1974. *The Story of New Mexico Mining, Scenic Trip No. 12*. Socorro: New Mexico Bureau of Mines and Mineral Resources.

Conkling, R.P., and M.B. Conkling. 1947. *The Butterfield Overland Mail, 1857–1869.* Glendale, Calif.: Arthur Clark.

Cremony, Captain John. 1868. *Life Among the Apaches.* Reprint. Tucson, Ariz.: Silhouettes (1954).

Debo, Angie. 1979. *Geronimo.* Norman: University of Oklahoma Press.

Geronimo. 1905. *Autobiography.* In *Geronimo—His Own Story*, ed. S.M. Barret. New York: Ballantine, 1973.

Hart, H.M. 1965. *Old Forts of the Southwest.* Seattle, Wash.: Superior Publishing Co.

Horgan, P. 1954. *Great River, the Rio Grande in North American History.* New York: Rinehart.

Lilley, Ben. 1981. *The Ben Lilley Legend.* Austin: University of Texas Press.

Lockwood, Frank C. 1938. *The Apache Indians.* New York: Macmillan.

Mails, Thomas E. 1974. *The People Called Apache.* Englewood Cliffs, N.J.: Prentice-Hall.

McKenna, James. 1965. *Black Range Tales.* New York: Rio Grande Press.

McFarland, E.F. 1974. *Wilderness of the Gila.* Albuquerque: University of New Mexico Press.

Ormsby, W.L. 1955. *The Butterfield Overland Mail.* San Marino, Calif.: Huntington Library.

Pattie, James O. 1984. *The Personal Narrative.* Lincoln: University of Nebraska Press.

Thrapp, Dan L. 1967. *The Conquest of Apacheria.* Norman: University of Oklahoma Press.

———. 1974. *Victorio and the Mimbres Apaches.* Norman: University of Oklahoma Press.

VII. MINERALS AND ROCKS

Hurlbut, C.S. 1970. *Minerals and Man.* New York: Random House.

Northrop, S.A. 1959. *Minerals of New Mexico.* Albuquerque: University of New Mexico Press.

Pough, F.H. 1960. *A Field Guide to Rocks and Minerals, Peterson Guide*. Boston: Houghton Mifflin.

VIII. PLANTS

Arnberger, L.P., and J.R. Janish. 1952. *Flowers of the Southwest Mountains*. Globe, Ariz.: Southwest Parks and Monuments Association.

Brockman, C.F. 1968. *Trees of North America, A Guide to Field Identification*. New York: Golden Press.

Clements, E.G. 1955. *Flowers of Mountains and Plains*. New York: H.W. Wilson.

Craighead, J.J., F.C. Craighead, and R.J. Davis. 1963. *A Field Guide to Rocky Mountain Wildflowers from Northern Arizona and New Mexico to British Columbia, Peterson Guide*. Boston: Houghton Mifflin.

Dodge, N.N. 1963. *100 Desert Wildflowers in Natural Color*. Globe: Southwest Parks and Monuments Association.

———. 1967. *100 Roadside Wildflowers of Southwest Uplands in Natural Color*. Globe: Southwest Parks and Monuments Association.

Dodge, N.N., and J.R. Janish. 1976. *Flowers of the Southwest Desert*. Globe: Southwest Parks and Monuments Association.

Elmore, F.H., and J.R. Janish. 1976. *Shrubs and Trees of the Southwest Uplands*. Globe: Southwest Parks and Monuments Association.

Little, E.L., Jr. 1960. *Southwestern Trees, A Guide to the Native Species of New Mexico and Arizona*. Reprinted 1976. U.S. Government Printing Office, Agriculture Handbook No. 9.

Patraw, P.M., and J.R. Janish. 1951. *Flowers of Southwest Mesas*. Globe: Southwest Parks and Monuments Association.

APPENDIX

Way high up in the Mogollons, if yuh ever camp there at
  night,
You'll hear a ruckus 'mongst the stones that'll raise your hair
  with fright;
You'll see a cow hoss come thunderin' by an' a lion trail
  along,
While the rider bold, with chin on high, sings forth his glory
  song.

"Oh glory be to me!" says he, "an' to my glory noose.
Oh pardner, tell my friends below I've took a ragin' dream in
  tow,
An' though I never laid him low, I'll never turn him loose!"
  —from the cowboy version of a ballad by Badger Clark,
    "poet lariat" of the West, written by him after an incident in
    a cattle camp in 1908. Later published by Harriet Monroe in
    Poetry magazine under the title "High-Chin Bob" as an
    "interesting example of an indigenous Western folk-song,"
    it can now be found in *Songs of the Cattle Trail and Cow
    Camp* by Alan Lomax.

Trail Mileages in the Gila Wilderness

The following mileages, compiled by the Forest Service, are for the most commonly traveled trails in the Gila Wilderness.

Trail Route	*Mileage*
TJ Corral to Gila Cliff Dwellings via West Fork	1.00
Gila Cliff Dwellings to Willow Creek via West Fork and Cub Mesa	33.25
Gila Cliff Dwellings to Hells Hole	12.75
Gila Cliff Dwellings to White Creek via West Fork	17.00
White Creek to Willow Creek via Cub Mesa and Turkeyfeather Pass	16.25
White Creek to Sandy Point via Cub Mesa and Turkeyfeather Pass	27.75
★Gila Cliff Dwellings to Willow Creek via West Fork	31.50
★White Creek to Willow Creek via West Fork and Turkeyfeather Pass	14.50
★White Creek to Sandy Point via West Fork and Turkeyfeather Pass	26.00
White Creek to Sandy Point via Mogollon Baldy and Crest Trail	23.00
White Creek to Mogollon Baldy	11.00
Mogollon Baldy to Hummingbird Saddle	7.25
Hummingbird Saddle to Sandy Point	4.75
Hummingbird Saddle to Redstone Park	5.00
Redstone Park to Whitewater Picnic Area	11.75
Little Creek Loop via Little Creek, Miller Spring, and Little Turkey Park	34.50
Woody's Corral to Little Creek	4.00
Little Creek at Trail #160 to Little Creek Spring	8.25
Little Creek Spring to Granite Peak	2.50
Little Creek Spring to Miller Spring Trail #159	6.75
Miller Spring Trail to Little Turkey Park	8.25

Little Turkey Park to Woody's Corral via Trail #160	7.33
Little Creek Spring to Sycamore Canyon via Turkey Creek	14.00
Little Creek Spring to Gila River via Turkey Creek	19.25
Woody's Corral to White Creek via Little Creek and McKenna Springs	21.00
Woody's Corral to McKenna Springs via Little Creek	16.00
McKenna Springs to White Creek via Trail #155	5.00
Woody's Corral to McKenna Park via Ring Canyon Trail #162 and #187	17.25
McKenna Park to White Creek via Horse Spring	3.25
TJ Corral to Middle Fork via Little Bear Canyon	4.25
TJ Corral to the Meadows via Big Bear Canyon	10.25
TJ Corral to Prior Cabin via Big Bear Canyon	12.00
Prior Cabin to Lilley Park	5.75
TJ Corral to White Creek via Woodland Park	22.50
TJ Corral to Woodland Park	12.50
Woodland Park to Lilley Park	6.75
Lilley Park to White Creek	3.25
White Creek to Middle Fork (Trotter) via Lilley Park	11.25
White Creek to Middle Fork (Flying V) via Lilley Park	11.75
Gila Cliff Dwellings to Meadows via Zig Zag and Big Bear Canyon	9.00
Gila Cliff Dwellings to Prior Cabin via Zig Zag and Woodland Park	11.75
Gila Cliff Dwellings to Prior Cabin via Zig Zag and Big Bear Canyon	10.75
Gila Visitor's Center to Snow Lake	36.00
Gila Visitor's Center to Little Bear Canyon via Middle Fork	6.50
Little Bear Canyon to the Meadows	8.50
The Meadows to Trotter	14.00
Trotter to Snow Lake	7.00
Upper Gila River Bridge to Turkey Creek via Gila River	32.00
Upper Gila River Bridge to Alum Camp	3.25
Alum Camp to Sapillo Creek	11.75
Sapillo Creek to Turkey Creek	17.00

Turkey Creek to White Creek via Sycamore and Turnbo
    Canyons   19.75
Little Creek to Trail #160   5.00
Little Creek to Little Turkey Park   9.25
Little Creek to Granite Peak   15.25

   *Not advised for livestock travel from White Creek to Cub Creek
through the West Fork Box.

A Guide to Wilderness Place Names

AIRPLANE MESA.   Claire Chenault of "Flying Tiger" fame crashed here while flying for the Army mail service. Ever since then it has been known as Airplane Mesa.

BEAR MOORE CABIN.   This cabin was the home of James "Bear" Moore, originally from St. Louis, a colorful local character whose face was seriously disfigured during a bear attack. Bear Moore Cave (on Big Turkey Creek) also acquired its name because of its use as a residence by "Bear" Moore. Because of his scarred face, he was quite reclusive and rarely seen by outsiders, living for the warm months of the year at his cabin on the West Fork and migrating to lower canyons in the winter (particularly to the mouth of Little Cherry Creek on Bear Creek north of Pinos Altos). Moore spent much of his time building traps for bears, which he would then kill, and prospecting for precious metals. Homer Pickens, a government trapper, discovered Moore's body while hunting mountain lions in January of 1924. The site was about six miles from Alum Camp on the Gila River, on the west side of Brushy Mountain, facing Little Creek. Moore had apparently broken his leg and then died from either shock or exposure after building a fire. Some cowboys from the Heart Bar Ranch, according to Woodrow, buried him just where they found his body.

BLOODGOOD CANYON.   This canyon was homesteaded by a family known as the Bloodgoods in the late nineteenth century and is named for them. The family still resides in southern New Mexico.

BLACK MOUNTAIN.   Apparently this mountain was named by the wife of pioneer cattleman Ben Kemp after the song entitled "The Black Hills of South Dakota," which she sang to her children.

CLAYTON CANYON AND CLAYTON MESA.   Both were named for an individual named Clayton, who ran cattle there in the late 1880s.

COONEY CANYON.   Woodrow reports he named this canyon for an old Civil War veteran, Captain Cooney, who disappeared while prospecting in the winter of 1914–15. His body was later found in the canyon that now bears his name and buried in Socorro. The lost gold mine for which he was searching in the canyon has never been found. It was originally discovered by a young surveyor who was killed by Indians before he could file a claim and have the site properly mapped and located.

COOPER CANYON.   This canyon is named for Alfred P. Cooper, who homesteaded on Iron Creek in 1880.

DOC CAMPBELL'S GILA HOT SPRINGS VACATION CENTER.   Doc Campbell, originally from Pennsylvania, has lived in the Gila country for 55 years, working first as a ranch hand and later purchasing the property where he now resides. He probably knows the Wilderness better than any other person. He has run cattle on it, worked as a fire lookout, taken countless pack trips into its backcountry, and served as official guide at the national monument as well as running his various business holdings. Several of his children, including Allen, now live and work in the valley.

GILA.   Gila (or "Helay" as it was sometimes called by the early pioneers) has one of three different sources: an Indian word *Xila*; a contraction of the Yuma Indian word *Hah-quah-sa-eel* (Running water which is salty); or the surname of the Spanish botanist Gilia who was in southwestern New Mexico in the late sixteenth century.

GRAVE CANYON.   This canyon is reportedly named for a fellow named Diaz, a companion of a man named Woods who was murdered with him and then buried here (see Grudging Cabin).

GRANITE PEAK.   Apparently the base rock of this peak appeared to be granite to the early pioneers. It is actually welded rhyolite tuff.

GRUDGING CABIN AND GRUDGING GRAVE.   According to Woodrow, the Grudging brother who maintained a cabin on the West Fork became involved in a disagreement with Tom Woods of the Middle Fork in the early 1890s. This subject of the dispute was a common one in the

West during this period: cattle stealing. The brothers eventually became so incensed by the loss of cattle, which they attributed to Woods, that they killed Woods's son and a Mexican man who resembled Tom Woods in a canyon of the Zig Zag Trail about one mile north of the West Fork. The feud then took an even worse turn as Tom Woods, in revenge, ambushed the brothers and killed Bill Grudging, who is buried behind the cabin where the gravestone now stands. Woods followed brother Tom Grudging to Louisiana, where, after hiding in a canebrake all night, he killed Tom when he came to his canoe at daylight. Despite the darkness, Woods recognized Tom Grudging by his disagreeable habit of spitting through the empty place where one of his front teeth had been. After hiding in the mountains for two years, Woods stood trial and was acquitted. He claimed in later years to have killed 14 men and to have the notches on his gun to prove it. Next to Bill Grudging is buried James Huffman, without a gravestone, who was shot by hired gun Buck Powell (whose real name was Murray) at the Huffman cabin near the mouth of EE Canyon. Huffman was known as a bully and Powell was acquitted. This also occurred in the 1890s, in the lawless period before statehood.

HALF MOON PARK.　This park is named for its resemblance to a half-moon.

HEART BAR.　This ranch, which was homesteaded in the early days, known then at the TJ, is now the property of the New Mexico Game and Fish Department. TJ Mesa, near the confluence of the Middle and West forks, is now the site for the local Forest Service headquarters, including the visitor's center. Several Indian ruins were excavated when the road and buildings were constructed.

IRON CREEK.　Iron Creek was named by Civil War veteran Thomas Wood, who while prospecting in the drainage discovered an iron vein crossing the creek above the Willow Creek Trail.

JERKY MOUNTAINS.　According to Woodrow, these mountains acquired their name when the Grudging brothers built a cabin two miles above the Heart Bar Ranch on the West Fork and another on the high ground between the headwaters of the West and East forks. From the latter location they would then make jerky or dried meat which they would later pack in to Mogollon to sell.

JOHNSON CANYON.   This canyon is named for law officer Keecheye Johnson, killed there after arresting one of the Jenks family, who resided at the confluence of White Creek and the West Fork, for stealing cattle. It is unknown who ambushed Johnson. After the incident Jenks rode over to Mogollon and turned himself into authorities on the cattle rustling charge.

LILLEY PARK.   Lilley, like Prior and Papenoe, settled in this country in the early 1880s, homesteading in what is now called Lilley Park, near Lilley Spring and Lilley Mountain. Papenoe was a French Canadian trapper. Killed by Apaches, Lilley's grave is close to Prior's grave on Clear Creek. Also killed in Apache raids were the McKenzie brothers from Ireland who had built a cabin at the confluence of White Creek and the West Fork. A short distance from their cabin a man named Baxter is buried, also killed by the Apaches. John C. Lilley, of Lilley Park, is not to be confused with Ben Lilly, a famous bear and lion hunter, originally from Louisiana, who spent many years hunting predators for local ranchers. Lilly was once requested as a hunting guide by Theodore Roosevelt because of his legendary stalking abilities. Lilly died late in 1936, two years before the great earthquakes rocked the Gila.

LOOKOUT MOUNTAIN.   Across Mogollon Creek from Shelley Peak is Lookout Mountain, so named because it was used by Geronimo as a sanctuary before he surrendered. Woodrow reports that "part of the old teepee ruins" could still be found earlier in the century in the canyons and on top of Lookout Point. Tepee Canyon, in the same area and running into Mogollon Creek, was reported by Stockbridge to be the refuge used by Geronimo in the winter of 1885–86. In his *Autobiography*, Geronimo alludes to a brief trip northward to the Warm Springs area at some period in the months before he finally surrendered to General Miles at Skeleton Canyon in southeastern Arizona. Stockbridge also reports tepee and camp "ruins."

THOMAS LYONS/LYONS LODGE.   Cattle baron Thomas Lyons built the famous Lyons Hunting Lodge near some hot springs on the East Fork as a gift for his bride, who is the grandmother of Ida Campbell, wife of Doc Campbell (see Doc Campbell's Gila Hot Springs Vacation Center). Teddy Roosevelt planned to visit and hunt at the lodge, but never made it. Although Thomas Lyons dreamed of extending his LC (Lyons/Campbell) cattle empire from the Rio Grande to the Arizona line, he never lived to see the ambition fulfilled. His murder, under very mysterious circumstances, is probably the great unsolved crime in southwestern New Mexico. The Lyons Lodge has been used as a guest resort since his death.

MCKENNA PARK.   Joe McKinney, a civil war veteran (not to be confused with James McKenna, the author of *Black Range Tales*), settled McKenna Park, which acquired its name because of some confusion in the similarity of McKinney's and McKenna's names. McKinney was one of the few survivors of the Battle of Soldier Hill, which occurred in December 1885 between Geronimo and the cavalry. The battlesite, which can be visited today, is located just off U.S. Highway 180 near Big Dry Creek. The creek in McKenna Park has also become known as McKenna Creek.

MCKENZIE GRAVE.   One of the two McKenzie brothers, both of whom were killed by the Apache, is buried just across White Creek near the confluence on the West Fork. The other McKenzie brother settled in Raw Meat Canyon, which got its name from a humorous incident involving two cowboys. They apparently stopped there and attempted to cook a quick meal but were unable to build a fire. They were so hungry that they simply ate their meat raw and gave the canyon that name.

MOGOLLON.   Mogollon, the name for the prominent mountain range in the western portion of the Gila Wilderness, has one of two possible sources: a descriptive reference by a Jesuit priest in 1675 which used the Spanish common noun *mogollon* (a hanger on, a parasite) with reference to the growths on the trees (possibly the lichen "Old Man's Beard" found in the spruce forests); or the Spanish governor of New

Mexico, Don Juan Ignacio Flores Mogollon, who served in that capacity from 1712 to 1715.

NAT STRAW CANYON.   This canyon is named for Robert Nelson "Nat" Straw, a bear and lion hunter originally from Minnesota, who as a boy of eight was captured and raised for a time by the Sioux Indians. He came to the Upper Gila in the 1890s and died in 1941 after a lifetime of exploring and prospecting. He claimed to know of ten thousand places "where the Lost Adams Diggings ain't," and to have written the following inscription on an aspen tree: "The Adams Diggings is a shadowy naught that lies in the valley of fanciful thought." Straw worked for many years as a hunter for the V Cross T, Flying V, Heart Bar, XSX, and over the vast sheep range of Eduardo Otero, claiming to bait bears only with scent, never with meat. Straw also claimed to have broken a grizzly bear to ride, using nothing more than a halter and rope reins. This yarn later appeared in an article entitled "Golden Liars of the Golden West" in *Vanity Fair* magazine in 1931, although Straw steadfastly defended the veracity of his tale.

OLD MILITARY ROAD.   This was a road constructed by the Army just after the Civil War. Parts of it are still visible along the East Fork and in the mountainous country south of the Lyons Lodge (see Military Trail #709 in the Mimbres District). For a time the Army had a small barracks at the Gila Hot Springs. The road spike later led several settlers up the East Fork. Farther up, just above the confluence with Spring Canyon, there are several graves bearing Spanish names.

PINOS ALTOS RANGE.   Pinos Altos comes from the Spanish meaning "tall pines."

PRIOR CABIN OR PRIOR PLACE.   Thomas C. Prior, who settled at a cabin now named for him between the Middle and West forks, was killed along with neighbors John Lilley and Presley Papence on a raid by the Apache in December 1885. He and Lilley were killed on Clear Creek and buried near an old cabin that used to stand there. Papenoe's grave, located where he fell, was about two miles north of Clear Creek on the trail to the Middle Fork (according to Woodrow).

SHELLEY PEAK AND SHELLEY PARK.   P.M. Shelley, who had driven a herd of cattle overland from Texas, homesteaded on the Mogollon Creek in the early 1880s. Shelley Peak and Shelley Park are both named for Shelley and his descendants, who continued to ranch in the area (according to Woodrow).

SNOW PARK.   This grassy park is so named because snow lingers there late into the spring.

Equipment in Primitive Areas

The following is a fairly complete list of recommended equipment to take with you into the Gila Wilderness Area.

I. Essential Equipment

Backpacking tent
Comfortable hiking boots (To avoid blisters use talcum or foot powder and wear light nylon socks beneath your heavier socks.)
Appropriate clothing (Carry sufficient clothing for the length and season of your trip. Dress in layers as temperatures fluctuate suddently throughout the year.)
Lightweight aluminum frame backpack and baffled goose or duck down sleeping bag
Gas stove (and extra fuel canister)
Sierra cup and eating bowl
Aluminum pan and handle
Aluminum pot and eating utensils
Two one-quart plastic water containers
Halozone tablets
Brillo pad and biodegradable soap
Waterproof matches and candles
Flashlight and extra batteries
Poncho
20 to 30 feet of 1/8" nylon cord
Pocket knife
Foam sleeping pad
First aid kit (Include Sunburn lotion and/or protective cream, Chapstick, moleskin, aspirin, Band-Aids, roll gauze, adhesive tape, and Ace bandage.)
Map (Standard 7-1/2-foot U.S.G.S. topographic maps are the best.)
Toothbrush and toothpaste
Toilet paper
G.I. can opener
Sunglasses and brimmed hat
Compass, mirror, and whistle
Emergency repair kit (needle, thread, wire, cord, screws)

Small towel
Comb

II. Optional Equipment

Camera and film
Fishing gear and license
Binoculars
Magnifying glass
Notebook and pencil, book to read
Vitamin tablets
Daypack (for side excursions)
Face mask or balaclava (winter travel)
Ice axe, crampons, climbing rope (winter travel)

III. Food Ideas (1–1.5 pound per day)

Standard freeze-dried foods
High energy foods (hard candy, nuts, dried fruit)
Instant soup, coffee, cocoa, hot chocolate, orange, and tomato juice
Pilot biscuits
Rice
Ramen noodles
Eggs (in hard plastic containers)
Spaghetti noodles (and powdered sauce)
Potato flakes
Canned tuna
Powdered milk
Hard sausage or pepperoni
Cheese and crackers
Jerky
Tortillas
Peanut butter and honey
Teabags and sugar
Oatmeal (with brown sugar and powdered milk)
Salt and pepper
Fresh trout
Fresh berries (in season)
Fresh nuts (in season)

Birds of the Gila Wilderness—A Field Checklist

Blackbird (Brewer's, Red-winged, Yellow-headed)
Bluebird (Mountain, Western)
Bunting (Lark)
Bushtit
Chat (Yellow-breasted)
Chickadee (Mountain)
Cowbird (Brown-headed)
Cuckoo (Yellow-billed)
Dove (Mourning)
Duck (Mallard, Common Merganser, Cinnamon Teal)
Eagle (Bald, Golden)
Finch (Cassin's, House)
Flycatcher (Ash-throated, Scissor-tailed)
Goldfinch (American, Lesser)
Grebe (Pied-billed)
Grosbeak (Black-headed, Blue, Evening)
Grouse (Pine)
Hawk (Cooper's, Mexican Black, Red-tailed, Sparrow)
Heron (Great Blue)
Hummingbird (Broad-tailed, Rufous)
Jay (Arizona, Piñon, Scrub, Steller's)
Junco (Gray-headed, Oregon)
Killdeer
Kingfisher (Belted)
Kinglet (Ruby-crowned)
Martin (Purple)
Mockingbird
Nighthawk
Nuthatch (Pygmy, White-breasted)
Oriole (Bullock's)
Osprey
Owl (Pygmy, Spotted)
Pewee (Wood)
Phoebe (Black, Say's)
Pigeon (Band-tailed)

Poor-will
Quail (Gambel's, Harlequin)
Raven (Common)
Redstart (Painted)
Roadrunner
Robin
Sandpiper (spotted)
Shrike (Loggerhead)
Siskin (Pine)
Solitaire (Townsend's)
Sparrow (Chipping, House, Lark, White-crowned)
Swallow (Barn, Cliff, Rough-winged, Tree, Violet-green)
Tanager (Cooper's, Western)
Thrasher (Curve-billed)
Titmouse (Bridled, Plain)
Towhee (Brown, Green-tailed, Spotted)
Turkey (Merriam's)
Vulture (Turkey)
Warbler (Audubon's, MacGillivray's, Red-faced, Wilson's, Yellow)
Whipporwill
Woodpecker (Acorn, Downy, Flicker, Hairy, Yellow-bellied Sap-
    sucker)
Wren (Bewick's, Canon, House)

This list was compiled from the author's field notes and from lists
furnished by the Forest Service, as well as from discussions with Doc
and Ida Campbell.

MAMMALS OF THE GILA WILDERNESS—A FIELD CHECKLIST

Antelope (Pronghorn)
Badger
Bats (Pallid, Silver-haired)
Bear (Black)
Beaver
Bobcat
Chipmunk (Cliff)
Coatimundi
Coyote
Deer (White-tailed, Mule)
Ferret
Fox (Gray)
Gopher (Pocket)
Jaguar
Javelina
Lion (Mountain)
Marten (Pine)
Marmot
Mink
Mouse (Brush, Field, Pocket, White-footed)
Muskrat
Porcupine
Prairie Dog
Rabbit (Cotton-tailed, Jack)
Raccoon
Rat (White-throated Wood)
Squirrel (Ground, Rock, Tassel-eared or Albert's)
Skunk (Spotted, Striped)
Vole (Meadow)
Wapiti (Elk)
Weasel

This list was compiled by the author.

AMPHIBIANS AND REPTILES OF THE GILA WILDERNESS— A FIELD CHECKLIST

SALAMANDERS	Tiger Salamander
SPADEFOOT TOADS	Couch's Spadefoot
	Western Spadefoot
	Plains Spadefoot
	Great Basin Spadefoot
TRUE TOADS	Woodhouse's Toad
	Southwestern Toad
	Red-spotted Toad
	Great Plains Toad
	Green Toad
TREE FROGS	Chorus Frog
	Canyon Tree Frog
	Arizona Tree Frog
TRUE FROGS	Leopard Frog
	Bullfrog
BOX TURTLES	Western Box Turtle
MUD TURTLES	Sonora Mud Turtle
SOFT SHELL TURTLES	Spiny Softshell
IGUANID LIZARDS	Lesser Earless Lizard
	Greater Earless Lizard
	Collard Lizard
	Crevice Spiny Lizard
	Clark's Spiny Lizard
	Eastern Fence Lizard
	Striped Plateau Lizard
	Side-blotched Lizard
	Tree Lizard
	Short-horned Lizard
SKINKS	Great Plains Skink
	Many-lined Skink
WHIPTAILS	New Mexico Whiptail
	Little Striped Whiptail
	Desert-Grassland Whiptail

	Chihuahua Whiptail
	Western Whiptail
ALLIGATOR LIZARD	Arizona Alligator Lizard
VENOMOUS LIZARDS	Gila Monster
SLENDER BLIND SNAKES	Texas Blind Snake
COLUBRID SNAKES	Ringneck Snake
	Coach Whip Snake
	Striped Whip Snake
	Western Patch-nosed Snake
	Mountain Patch-nosed Snake
	Gopher or Bull Snake
	Common King Snake
	Sonora Mountain King Snake
	Narrow-Headed Garter Snake
	Western Terrestrial Garter Snake
	Black-necked Garter Snake
	Checkered Garter Snake
	Western Ground Snake
	Western Black-headed Snake
	Plains Black-headed Snake
	Night Snake
CORAL SNAKES	Arizona Coral Snake (venomous)
VIPERS (VENOMOUS)	Western Diamondback Rattlesnake
	Rock Rattlesnake
	Black-tailed Rattlesnake
	Western Rattlesnake

Note. Most of the snakes and other reptiles found in the wilderness will be harmless. Many, such as the bull snake, which preys not only on small rodents but also on rattlesnakes, are extremely important animals in the ecosystem. Snakebites occur most often when inexperienced people are trying to kill or to catch snakes. There is no faster striking poisonous snake in the world than the rattlesnake. Its venom is extremely poisonous and can be fatal. Leave *all* snakes alone and stay away from areas where they are commonly found.

All horned lizards (horned toads) are protected. It is illegal to kill, collect, sell, or take them from the State of New Mexico.

All bullfrogs are also protected in this area.

This inventory resulted from a biological survey of various life forms made by Dr. B.J. Hayward, Western New Mexico University, Silver City.

Fish of the Gila Wilderness—A Field Checklist

SALMON (TROUT)	Gila Trout (endangered)
	Rainbow Trout (originally from Pacific streams)
	Brown Trout (originally from Europe)
	Eastern Brook Trout (originally from eastern United States)
SUCKERS	Gila Sucker
	Rio Grande Mountain Sucker
	Gila Mountain Sucker
MINNOWS	Bonytail
	Longfin Dace
	Flathead Chub
	Speckled Dace
	Loach Minnow
	Spike Dace
	Gila Topminnow
CATFISH	Yellow Bullhead
	Flathead
	Black Bullhead
	Channel Catfish
SUNFISH	Largemouth black bass
	Smallmouth black bass
	Bluegill

This inventory resulted from a biological survey of various life forms made by Dr. B.J. Hayward, Western New Mexico University, Silver City.

Common Plants of the Gila Wilderness—A Field Checklist

Agave (Palmer)
Alder (New Mexican)
Algerita
Alumroot
Ash (Mountain)
Aster
Bareley (Foxtail)
Beargrass
Bee-balm
Bluebells
Boxelder (Inland)
Buffalo Gourd
Cactus (Yellow Prickly Pear)
Camas (Death)
Cattail
Chokecherry
Cinquefoil
Clematis
Cliff Rose
Clover (White)
Columbine
Coneflower
Cottonwood
Currant (Golden)
Creeper (Virginia)
Cypress (Arizona)
Dandelion
Datil
Datura (Sacred)
Dock
Elderberry
Fern
Fir (Douglas)

Firewheel
Fleabane
Four o'clock
Gernaium
Gilia (Scarlet)
Grape (Wild)
Groundsel
Harebell (Blue)
Hemlock (Water)
Hoptree (Narrowleaf)
Ivy (Poison)
Lily (Mariposa)
Loco Weed
Locust (New Mexican)
Lupine
Madrone (Arizona)
Manzanita (Pointleaf)
Maple (Bigtooth)
Mahogany (Mountain)
Mallow (Globe)
Meadow Rue
Mesquite
Mescale
Monkey Flower (Yellow)
Morning Glory
Mullein
Oak (Emory, Gambel's, Gray)
Olive (Wild)
Onion (Wild)
Orchid (11 Species)
Paintbrush (Red Indian)
Penstemon
Phlox

Pine (Piñon, Ponderosa,
  Chihuahua, Apache)
Poppy (Prickly)
Potato (Wild)
Primrose (Evening Yellow)
Raspberry (Wild)
Rye (Wild)
Rush (Scouring)
Saltbrush
Sedge
Shooting Star
Solomon's Seal (False)
Smartweed
Spring Beauty

Spider Flower
Spruce (Englemann's)
Strawberry (Wild)
Stonecrop
Sunflower
Sumac
Sycamore (Arizona)
Tule
Violet
Yarrow
Yucca (Schott's)
Willow (Pacific)
Walnut (Arizona)
Watercress

This list was compiled by the author and is not meant to be exhaustive.

Important Addresses and Information

Supervisor's Office
Gila National Forest
2601 North Silver Street
Silver City, New Mexico 88061
388-8201

Glenwood Ranger Station
Gila National Forest
P.O. Box 8
Glenwood, New Mexico 88039
539-2481

Silver City Ranger District
Gila National Forest
2915 Hwy 180 East
Silver City, New Mexico 88061
538-2771

Mimbres Ranger Station
Gila National Forest
Box 79, Mimbres, New Mexico 88049
536-2250

Wilderness Ranger Station
Gila National Forest
Route 11, Box·100
Silver City, New Mexico 88061
536-9344/9461

Topographic maps should always be used for wilderness travel. They may be purchased directly from local sporting goods stores or from the U.S. Geological Survey at the following address: U.S.G.S. Map Store, Box 25286, Denver Federal Center, Denver, Colorado 80225. The following 7-1/2 foot quadrangles cover the Gila Wilderness in its entirety (they currently cost $2.25 per sheet, so care should be exercised in their selection. A map guide is availabe from the U.S.G.S. to aid in that process): Mogollon, Bearwallow Mountain, Negrito Mountain, Loco Mountain, Canyon Creek Mountains, Black Mountain, Spring Canyon, Holt Mountain, Grouse Mountain, Mogollon Baldy Peak, Lilley Mountain, Woodland Park, Burnt Corral Canyon, Wall Lake, Moon Ranch, Rice Ranch, Shelley Peak, Diablo Range, Little Turkey Park, Gila Hot Springs, Middle Mesa, Buckthorn, Canteen Canyon, Canyon Hill, Granny Mountain, Copperas Peak, and North Star Mesa. The trail maps in this book are from the new U.S.G.S. 1:100,000 metric topographical map. They are $4.50 each and have a 50 meter contour interval. It's recommended that a U.S.G.S. map showing the entire Gila Wilderness be used together with a U.S.F.S. Gila Wilderness map, which sells for $2.00.

Resolution

Submitted by the Resolutions Committee at the Annual Meeting of the New Mexico–Arizona Section of the Wildlife Society on February 2, 1973, in Farmington, New Mexico

Pertaining to the Reintroduction of Grizzly Bear into Arizona and New Mexico

Whereas, grizzly bears formerly occupied large areas of Arizona and New Mexico, and

Whereas, grizzly bears have been completely extirpated from Arizona and New Mexico since the 1930s; and

Whereas, there remain large areas of suitable habitat in Arizona and New Mexico in public ownership within the former distribution of grizzly bears; and

Whereas, the New Mexico–Arizona Section of the Wildlife Society is of the philosophy that species diversity and reintroduction of native fauna are desirable; and

Whereas, the grizzly bear was and could be a desirable complement to our faunal realm; and

Whereas, grizzly bears are currently available for reintroduction from areas in the continental United States in and adjacent to lands administered by the National Park Service; and

Whereas, the New Mexico–Arizona Section of the Wildlife Society recognizes the inherent problem of anticipated or actual incompatability of grizzly bears with livestock operations;

Now therefore, be it resolved that the New Mexico–Arizona Section of the Wildlife Society encourages the administrators of the United States Forest Service lands possessing wilderness characteristics, designated or de facto, within the historical range of grizzly bear in Arizona and/or New Mexico to prepare management and contingency plans to provide for the successful reintroduction of this species in limited numbers and area.[1]

[1]After considerable discussion the resolution was adopted 23 to 17.

Evaluation of the Gila Wilderness for Re-establishment of the Grizzly Bear

Albert W. Erickson, Ph.D.
Wildlife Management Associates
Bellevue, Washington
and
College of Fisheries
University of Washington, Seattle

September, 1974

Abstract

An evaluation of the Gila Wilderness was made to assess the suitability of the area for the reintroduction of the grizzly bear. This evaluation led to the conclusion that the approximate 300 square miles contained in the Gila Wilderness was sufficiently large to satisfy the spatial requirements of a small population of grizzlies. The habitat of the area was also deemed suitable for fulfilling the food, cover and denning requirements of the species although the current habitat array was believed less attractive for the grizzly than at the time of the species extirpation from the area in the 1930's. The direction of the change was a reduction in the amount of open areas and the development of a closed canopy forest due to intense fire control. As consequence of this, the amount of grasses and early successional plants upon which the grizzly depends for its food appears to be in a declining state.

The attractiveness of the Gila Wilderness as grizzly habitat is judged equivalent to the areas where the species exists in the national forests of the mountain states. As such the Gila Wilderness is perhaps at best only moderately good habitat for grizzlies on a comparison with areas such as Kodiak Island or the Alaska Peninsula.

While it is probable that a successful reintroduction of the grizzly into the Gila Wilderness can be achieved, it seems probable that some direct conflict can be expected between livestock grazing use of the

Wilderness and the grizzly. Suggestions for reducing this potential conflict are (1) stock reductions in prime grizzly habitats, (2) shifting stocks at critical season, and (3) purposeful control of bears in problem areas.

Recommended habitat management for the grizzly in the Wilderness include (1) directed use of wild fire to create openings and suppress forest regeneration and (2) the creation of unattractive vegetative buffers between prime grizzly habitat and grazing areas.

Recommendations are also given relative to stocking procedures should an introduction be attempted.

INTRODUCTION

This report presents an evaluation of the suitability of the Gila Wilderness of the Gila National Forest for reintroduction of the grizzly bear [*Ursus arctos horribilus*] and presents recommendations as to methodology and management, should an introduction be attempted.

The study was performed under U.S. Forest Service Contract Number 6-369-74 awarded to the author on March 25, 1974. The broad objectives of the study were as follows:

1. To delineate the boundaries of an area within which grizzly bear habitat management could be effected.
2. To identify existing and potential seasonal key grizzly bear habitat within the area established and propose management for these areas.
3. To qualify or rate this grizzly bear habitat with that located throughout the United States, including Alaska.

METHODS

The methodology employed in the development of this report concerned (1) a review of maps and information on the Gila Wilderness, provided by Gila National Forest, (2) a search of literature pertinent to the study objectives, (3) a 5 day field reconnaissance of the Gila Wilderness, and (4) discussions of the project with officials of the Gila National Forest and the New Mexico Department of Fish and Game.

The Forest materials examined included:

1. Grazing allotment map of the Gila Forest, including the Gila Wilderness . . .
2. Vegetative type map of the Gila Wilderness . . .
3. Fire history map of the Gila Wilderness for the period 1961–1970
4. Area maps
5. Check lists of the plants, avifauna, mammals and herbs occurring in the Gila Wilderness.

The field reconnaissance was performed during the period April 5–11, 1974. The effort entailed first an aerial examination of the Gila Wilderness and adjacent areas in the company of New Mexico Department of Fish and Game Officials Messrs. William Huey, Asst. Director and Richard Brown, Pilot–Conservation Officer.

This reconnaissance provided the contractor orientation and a first approximation of the Gila Wilderness as grizzly bear habitat, particularly the general physiognomy of the area, spatial relationships and area use considerations.

A 4 day horseback trip approximating 80 trail miles was subsequently made into the core of the Gila Wilderness. . . . Personnel participating in this trip and advisory to the contractor were, Mr. Dale Jones, Wildlife Biologist USFS Region 3, Mr. John Ross, Wildlife Biologist, and Mr. Jack Carter, Asst. Ranger, Gila National Forest; Mr. Robert Welch, Game Biologist, and Mr. Hugh Bishop, Conservation Officer, New Mexico Department of Fish and Game; and Mr. John Phelps, Game Biologist of the Arizona Department of Fish and Game.

On this trip, judgements were made of the areas traversed as to their attractiveness as grizzly bear habitat and searches were made for evidence of black bear sign. Particular attention was given in the field effort to judge the suitability of the Gila Wilderness area as grizzly habitat on the basis of both current management and stage of plant succession and possible later use and future successional stages. Consideration was also given to evidence of past, present and possible future Forest management practices as 1) bearing on the attractiveness of the Gila Wilderness as grizzly habitat, and 2) the value of that use relative to that if the grizzly were a species to be given prime management consideration in the Gila Wilderness.

Past Evidence of the Distribution and Abundance of the Grizzly in the Gila Wilderness

Only cursory information exists of the grizzly bear in the Gila Wilderness despite the apparent fact that the species was once judged to be so numerous as to constitute a serious menace to human life and domestic stock (Bailey, 1931). That the species has been extant in the Gila Forest since the establishment of the Gila Wilderness in 1924 seems reasonably certain, although it appears that the species was exterminated from the area by the early 1930's. At the turn of the century, the grizzly bear had already been largely exterminated from the state, principally due to a coordinated and concerted control effort by ranchers (Bailey, 1931). The main residual areas where the species was to be found included the Mimbres, Mogollon and San Francisco Ranges. In 1910 the Forest Service reported grizzlies as still extant in the Taos, San Juan and Gallinas Mountains.

The first concerted attempt to assess the status of the waning grizzly population in New Mexico was by J. S. Ligon, who in a report prepared for the U.S. Forest Service in May of 1917, estimated a state population of 48 grizzly bears and presented a map depicting their distribution. Two of these residuum lie within or impinge upon the Gila Wilderness. In a subsequent report presented in 1927, Ligon stated that the predatory habits of the grizzly had resulted in their almost total extermination from the state.

Evaluation of the Gila Wilderness as Grizzly Habitat

Three prime considerations bear on the suitability of the Gila Wilderness as habitat currently or potentially suitable for the grizzly bear. These include (1) the spatial sufficiency of the area to satisfy the normal mobility traits of the species, (2) the support capability of the area for the grizzly and (3) the compatability of the grizzly with other resource uses of the area. These three considerations are not independent, of course, but an attempt will be made to examine each in this analysis.

SPATIAL SUFFICIENCY. Not surprisingly, there is not a large body of data detailing the movement traits and home range sizes of brown bears.[1] Sufficient information exists, however, to permit the judgement that the normal movements of grizzly bears are quite limited, despite popularly held views to the contrary. Radio-tracking studies conducted on Kodiak Island by Berns and Hensel (1972) determined that 14 radio-tracked bears confined their principle [*sic*] activities to an average area of only 5.5 square miles. The average maximum between-point movements of these animals was 12.5 linear miles (range 5.0 to 29.4). The maximum movements between points were usually associated with movements between winter dens and the major summer activity centers.

In a study of grizzly bears in the Yukon Territory, Pearson (1972) reported the average home range size of eight female grizzlies as 27 square miles and that of an unstated number of males as 114 square miles. Craighead and Craighead (1962) reported the home range of 10 radioed Yellowstone grizzlies of mixed sexes and ages as averaging 41.9 square miles. The maximum and minimum ranges of these animals were 8 and 168 square miles, respectively.

The spatial requirement of grizzly bears can further be inferred from the minimum sizes of areas where the species persists in relic status. Noteworthy among these populations are the 19 to 20 insular populations extant in Europe (Curry-Lindahl, 1972). Most of these populations occupy areas less expansive than that present in the portion of the Gila Wilderness closed to cattle. Notable among these is a population of 60 to 80 bears occurring in the Abruzzo National Park in the Apennines. This park is only 250 square miles in area or slightly smaller than the non-grazed portion of the Gila Wilderness. Correspondingly, a relic population of approximately 15 bears exists in a 200 square mile area in Norway (Elkmork, 1962). Other examples exist in Asia and in the Americas. The most significant of these as concerns the present study are two relic populations of bears reported as existing in Mexico (Leopold, 1967 and 1969). One of these populations exists in the Sierra del Nido, a small, isolated range emerging from the desert of central Chihuahua. This population was apparently sustaining itself in an area of only 5000 acres (Cowan, 1972, page 531)

[1]The grizzly is but one sub-form of the European-Asian and American brown bear (*Ursus arctos*).

until subjected to a campaign of extermination (Leopold, 1969). The second population exists in the upper Yaqui Basin of Sonora in the Sierra Madre about 100 miles west of the Sierra del Nido (Leopold, 1969). Of the grizzly stocks remaining today, these populations most probably represent the race of grizzly most close genetically and habitat-wise to the stock type which formerly occupied the Gila Wilderness.

The foregoing records suggest that the approximately 360 square miles of area contained in the Gila Wilderness are sufficient to fulfill the spatial needs of at least a small grizzly population, assuming, of course, that the area is suitable grizzly habitat.

HABITAT EVALUATION. Inasmuch as the habitat requirements of the grizzly bear are ill-defined (Erickson, 1974), and no hard analytical data exist on the habitat characteristics of the Gila Wilderness, only a judgemental evaluation may be made of the attractiveness of the Wilderness as habitat for the grizzly bear. The generalized type map of the Gila Wilderness shows the Wilderness as fairly well broken into an intermixed array of eight major vegetative types based on dominant species. . . . The preponderant vegetative type is Ponderosa pine which covers the principle [sic] high country. The second prominent vegetative type is mixed conifer which together with spruce-fir forests occupies the remaining non–Ponderosa pine high country. The lower ranges and the periphery of the Wilderness area contain a large component of pinyon-juniper with major components of brush.

Conspicuously limited in abundance in the Wilderness are the grass and aspen vegetative types. . . .

Observations during the reconnaissance led me to conclude that the grassland and pioneer vegetative component of the Gila Wilderness was today quite limited in extent over that present in the recent past. This conclusion is premised on three observations. The first of these was the major invasion of prime grassland meadows by forest types. . . . The second was the seeming replacement of a grass-type understory beneath the Ponderosa forests by shrubs and forest regeneration which often assumed the character of a dog-hair thicket. Lastly was the near absence of the aspen type. Each of these observations supports the view that the vegetative character of the forest today is markedly different from that of earlier times. The prime cause for the change appears to have been intense fire control. The effectiveness of this control is apparent by reference to the fire map. . . , which shows literally hundreds of fire starts. Despite this, evidence of recent fire in the Wilderness during our field reconnaissance was essentially nil. The seeming result of this intense fire control has been a marked diminishment of the grassland area within the Wilderness. Whereas this type appears formerly to have been maintained as a fire dis-climax in forest openings and beneath Ponderosa stands, the absence of suppressing fire has permitted understory shrub and mixed-age stand development.

Assuming the foregoing to be true, does the current vegetative pattern render the Gila Wilderness more or less attractive as grizzly bear habitat? In my opinion, the Wilderness as currently vegetated is markedly less attractive as grizzly habitat than it would be if grasses and herbaceous growth were more prominent features. While no definitive habitat studies of the grizzly have been made, there is little doubt that the species thrives best and reaches its greatest densities in those areas of its range wherein grasses and herbaceous plants constitute a significant component of the vegetative array (Erickson, 1974). Conversely, there is to my knowledge not a single population of brown bears in areas of heavy forests which could be considered abundant on a comparison with those populations found in grassland habitats such as exist on Kodiak Island or on the Alaska Peninsula.

As concerns the Gila Wilderness, it seems unlikely that heavy populations of grizzlies ever existed in the Wilderness proper and it is very likely that the heaviest populations in the area formerly occurred in the foothills. In this regard, I was struck during the field reconnaissance at the attractiveness of the Jordan Mesa as grizzly habitat. This area lies at the northeast edge of the Gila Wilderness in the area currently under consideration for addition to the Gila Wilderness. The area possesses a large grassland component, well interspersed with forest types. . . .

If the judgement is correct that the current vegetative state of the Gila is less attractive as grizzly habitat than during former times, does it follow that the Gila Wilderness is presently unsuitable habitat for the grizzly? In my opinion, this would be exceedingly unlikely. Even in its current state, the Gila Wilderness possesses meadows, openings and pioneer areas equalling or exceeding those extant in other areas where grizzly populations exist. Among these are the populations occurring throughout Southeastern Alaska and in many National Forest areas of the Northwest, notably the Bob Marshall Wilderness. Further, the associated food base extant in the Gila Wilderness appeared significantly more abundant in both abundance and type as compared to the food resources available to more northerly grizzly bear populations. The plant list for the Gila Wilderness numbers 53 species of grasses, 195 herbaceous species, 50 shrubs and 63 tree species (Hayward, et al. 1974). This vast array of potential plant food items is impressive. Beyond the grasses and herbaceous plants foraged upon heavily by bears as the basic food staple, I was impressed during the field reconnaissance at the abundance of fruit bearing plants. Prominent among these was the abundance of pinyon–juniper berries along the lower fringes of the Wilderness zones traversed. These berries are apparently retained almost year long at certain sites and constituted the bulk of the black bear scats observed during the reconnaissance trip. Reports in the literature identify these berries as important foods of the grizzly in former times (Bailey, 1931). Another prominent food available to bears in the Gila Wilderness is acorn mast. Despite the recognized inconsistency of acorn mast production, the presence of eight oak species suggests that some production of acorn mast can be expected as a regular occurrence. The field reconnaissance revealed oaks as a prominent tree type and examination of the trees and ground areas for acorn shell remains revealed that 1973 had been a good mast year. While the dependability of this food item is unknown, the fact that eight oak species exist in the area provides some assurance that at least some mast can be expected each year. A further mast item is pinyon nuts, although the frequency of a significant crop is apparently quite irregular. A number of Rosaceae were also observed during the field reconnaissance, particularly service berry and choke cherry, and whenever present they are avidly fed upon by bears.

Other food items of significance likely included the fruit of the prickly pear and yucca present in the lower fringe area of the Wilderness. Another likely important food item is the fruit of manzanita (little apple) which is mentioned in early accounts as eaten by grizzly bears (Bailey, 1931).

In assessing the attractiveness of the Gila Wilderness as grizzly habitat one must of course consider the year-long character of the area. At the season of the field reconnaissance, the region was exceedingly dry except at the higher elevations. It seems likely, therefore, that the grizzlies formerly occupying the Gila Wilderness area may have exhibited seasonal range shifts as has been reported for grizzly bear populations recently studied by radio telemetry (Berns and Hensel, 1972; Craighead and Craighead, 1969; and Pearson, 1972). In the Gila, it is probable that the bears either migrated to the high country or congregated along water courses during the dry season. Likely, both circumstances prevailed. It is probable also that most of the grizzlies migrated to the high country in the late fall due to the propensity of the species to seek high areas for denning (Craighead and Craighead, 1972 and Lentfer, et al., 1972). A migration to the low country was also a likely event upon arousal as the animals sought food during the meager spring period.

The consequence of these distributional shifts will be discussed beyond.

The suitability of the Gila Wilderness as satisfying the cover, shelter and denning requirements of the grizzly, is a foregone conclusion, in my opinion.

CONFLICT PROBLEMS.   A prime consideration bearing on the suitability of the Gila Wilderness as suitable habitat for the grizzly concerns potential conflicts between the species and other uses of the Wilderness. The obvious and critical factor is the potential conflict of the bears with livestock interests. The current Gila Wilderness comprises an area of approximately 360 square miles of which approximately 300 square miles is closed to livestock grazing. The area closed to grazing measures approximately 13 × 25 miles and encloses the central core high country. As assessed earlier, this block of country is sufficient to satisfy the spatial needs of at least a small population of bears and the habitat of the Gila Wilderness would appear to satisfy the food requirements of the grizzly as well. Despite that adjudged suitability of the area spatially and as grizzly habitat, it would be unrealistic to conclude that the bears would not leave the confines of the Wilderness. This happy state could be expected only if the Wilderness were inclusive of all the area attractive to bears and the fate of the original stock is profound evidence to the contrary. It is assumed, therefore, that some movement of grizzlies can be expected into the portion of the Gila Wilderness open to grazing and into adjacent non-wilderness portions of the forest.

Table 1 presents data provided to the contractor on stocking rates on the portion of the Wilderness open to grazing. These data show that approximately 1400 head of stock are grazed 8 to 12 months a year on that portion of the Gila Wilderness open to grazing. Another 900 head of stock are grazed on the Jordan Mesa, Indian Creek and Canyon Creek allotments adjacent to the Gila Wilderness on the northeast. While not given, equivalent stocking rates can be assumed on the Reading Mountain and Redstone allotments to the southeast, on the Shelton Canyon allotment to the west, and on the T-Bar and 625 allotments to the north. These stock allotments abutting directly upon the non-grazed portion of the Gila Wilderness would undoubt-edly experience some livestock depredation should the grizzly bear be successfully stocked in the Gila Wilderness. Much of this area is proposed for addition to the Gila Wilderness. The degree of potential

TABLE 1. *Grazing Quotas for the Gila Wilderness and Adjacent Forest Areas*

Allotments	Stock Type		Period		AUM
Wilderness					
803 Rain Creek	302 cattle and	6 horses	8¼ months		2530
801 Davis Canyon	175 cattle and	5 horses	8	months	1440
804 Rough Canyon	63 cattle and	4 horses	12	months	804
802 Mogollon Creek	31 cattle and	4 horses	2½ months		298
807 Watson Mtn.	123 cattle and	5 horses	12	months	1536
800 Brock Canyon	123 cattle and	5 horses	12	months	1524
806 Spar Canyon	165 cattle		12	months	1980
808 XSX	300 cattle and	10 horses	12	months	3720
Hulse		13 horses	12	months	156
Hage		10 horses	12	months	120
Campbell		27 horses	12	months	175
Adjacent area					
103 Canyon Creek	97 cattle		12	months	1164
105 Indian Creek	150 cattle		12	months	1800
106 Jordan Mesa	580 cattle		12	months	6960

conflict undoubtedly could be minimized, however, according to how the bears were managed and when and how livestock were grazed in the Wilderness (see beyond). The level of the predational conflict is naturally difficult to judge, but I would think that it might approximate that experienced with the cougar. Evidence of this predator was observed during the field study and whatever predational loss being experienced is apparently tolerable.

Other potential conflicts of the grizzly bear with other uses of the Gila Wilderness concern principally direct conflicts with human recreational use of the Wilderness. The portent of this conflict exists in direct relation to the type and management of the recreation use. Greatest conflict can be expected in areas subjected to heavy picnicking or camping. Garbage from these activities attracts bears and almost invariably the animals develop nuisance tendencies. A consequence of this is a buildup of bear-human incidents which is usually resolved by stringent actions being taken against the bears (witness the Yellowstone and Glacier parks situations). The net result is a constant wasteful drain on the bear population. The solution is, of course, stringent garbage management particularly in areas heavily and regularly impacted by human use.

While I am aware of the existence of garbage dumps in or adjacent to the Wilderness, it should be mentioned also that such sites will pull bears for considerable distances with the same consequences noted above. Further, the wilderness image of the species is diminished when the species is observed in the role of a skid row bum.

SUMMARY EVALUATION.   As was indicated in evaluating the habitat character of the Gila Wilderness and the spatial requirements of the grizzly bear, the Gila Wilderness is deemed sufficiently large and capable of providing resource support for at least a small population of grizzly bear. At the same time, there is the near-certainty of some conflict between grizzly bears and other uses, notably livestock grazing, of the Gila Wilderness and Forest, should the grizzly be introduced. The extent of this potential conflict can only be surmised and would be influenced by management practices. Assuming an introduction of the grizzly were to be made, the management options as regards this conflict are four. The first would be to simply permit the normal evolution of events, which might prove tolerable with reasonable accommodations between stock interest and the Forest. The second possibility would be reduced grazing use of the Gila Wilderness and Forest where this use resulted in the development of a problem with bears. A third management option would be to stringently control bears when they impinged upon stock grazing areas. The last alternative would concern a blend of options two and three wherein consideration would be weighted favorably toward the bears in areas of chronic or high attraction for the species and conversely, the bears would be suppressed in areas of low attraction.

With accommodation, the exercise of option four might not prove as grievous as would first appear to be the case. In the first instance, it may very well develop that possible depredations of livestock by bears could be greatly diminished by withholding stock from the range during critical periods. In my experience with this problem on Kodiak Island, the time of principle [sic] conflict was in the early spring when the bears migrated to the low lands. Young stock is, of course, particularly vulnerable at this time. Obviously, this conflict could be significantly averted by withholding stock from the range until the bears had moved back to higher elevations or into other areas.

On the flip side of the coin and assuming a bear population buildup, it would seem only practical to direct control or exploitation of bear stocks into areas of the range where conflicts are likely to manifest themselves. During the initial buildup of the bear population, this control might assume the form of actual control actions. Later hunting could be directed into these areas. Particularly to be recommended would be a spring bear season running from normal pre-denning emergence beyond the time of likely predational expression. Such a season would serve to arrest the spread of bears beyond the boundaries desired by 1) removal of surpluses and 2) by displacement harassment.

THE FEASIBILITY OF AN INTRODUCTION. Should it be decided that a reintroduction of the grizzly bear into the Gila Wilderness was a viable consideration, the question remains as to the form of the introduction and the type and availability of grizzly bears for the stocking attempt. The following discussion addresses these questions.

RACE TYPES AND THEIR AVAILABILITY. As indicated earlier in this report, the relic grizzly bear populations occurring in Mexico are in greatest likelihood the most similar habitat-wise and genetically to the grizzly population formerly occurring in the Gila Wilderness. Ideally, these populations would be the most desired source from which to obtain animals for introduction into the Gila Wilderness. It is questionable that this race will survive for any lengthy period, however, in view of the persecution the remaining populations are experiencing. On the other hand, there is the possibility that certain of these animals exist in captivity and the possibility of obtaining specimens for introduction from this source should be explored. Beyond this consideration, any of a number of grizzly stocks should be suitable for introduction and obtaining suitable animals for stocking should not be too difficult. Such animals could be specifically trapped or obtained as surpluses from zoological gardens.

There would appear to be some advantage in obtaining grizzlies for stocking from populations occurring in areas where the animals have been subjected to control or harassment pressures once they leave the confines of core mountainous areas. Bears from such areas would seemingly already have begun behavioral adaptations toward survival in marginal and confined habitats due to survival selection. While it could be argued that practically all of the grizzly stocks in the Americas, except Alaska, are of this type, I would suggest that those populations occurring in multiple-use forests would be the most likely to manifest such selection to the greatest degree. Less so would be those populations in areas such as national parks where the species associates with man in near-impunity on one hand and on the other faces animosity and persecution.

While obtaining grizzlies for stocking from an area such as the Bob Marshall Wilderness would be somewhat more difficult than obtaining stock from other sources, the end result might well be worth the increased cost and effort.

OTHER STOCKING CONSIDERATIONS. Likely to be important to the success of any stocking attempt, are factors concerning the ages, sexes and character of the animals to be released and when, where and how the releases might best be made. In my opinion, it would be foolhardy to use nuisance animals obtained from other areas, particularly national parks, as stock for introductions. The fact that the animals are nuisances elsewhere makes it a near-certainty they will be a cause of difficulties when again released. The prime argument for the use of these animals is their ready availability and the fact that there is little other use for the animals. These considerations shrink in significance when one considers the jeopardy the use of such animals could have on an introductory effort which can be expected to be most controversial, no matter how professionally performed.

As concerns the sexes and ages of bears to be used for introduction, I would suggest that best success would be realized if the animals stocked were either young (yearlings or 2-year olds), pregnant females or females with accompanying cubs. In truly wild bear populations, females and young are quite wary and consequently appear less inclined to become problem animals (Erickson, 1964).

As concerns the best time of the year for a release, I would suggest the fall fruit-producing period. Food type and abundance should be greatest at this time and thus the animals would not have to roam widely to satisfy their food needs. Further, the propensity of the grizzly to seek den sites in high areas (Craighead and Craighead, 1972; and Lintfer et al., 1972) would seemingly orient them into the mountains of the Gila Wilderness immediately following the fall foraging season as opposed to areas off the Wilderness.

As concerns the site of any release, it follows that a release near the center of the Wilderness would be preferable to a release on the periphery of the Wilderness. Such a release could be easily accomplished by helicopter transport of bears in an anesthetized state. The procedures of capture, anesthetization and transport of bears are in a technically advanced state and the physical aspects of release should be able to be accomplished with a minimum difficulty unless encumbered by red tape.

POST TRANSPLANT MONITORING.   A component aspect of any responsible attempt to transplant the grizzly into the Gila Wilderness would include the provision for close assessment of the releases. This could be accomplished most accurately by marking and radio-tagging all released bears. While the simple tag marking of released bears would provide quite close assessment of the ultimate fate of a majority of the released bears, little information would be developed on the move-

ments and actions of the animals during the critical period immediately following release. This could be accomplished only by radio
telemetry whereby the animals could be easily monitored as to general location with aircraft and subsequently monitored from the
ground as feasible. The efficacy of this procedure is the fact that hard
information would exist concerning the locations and actions of the
released bears and thus wild speculations could be curbed or ad-
dressed factually. Secondly, should a released animal fail to establish
itself suitably, either spatially or habit-wise, it could quite likely be
easily located and a recovery effort made. While there would appear
to be limited virtue to the non-fatal recovery of an undesirable transplant animal, a live recovery could seemingly be accomplished either
by intense trappling following radio-location or the animal could be
bayed with dogs and captured with a syringe gun. It is possible too,
that released animals could be harassed when they approached off-
limit areas and thus be conditioned to avoid such areas. A further
virtue of the radio-technique as employed on bears is the possibility of
annual re-instrumentation of the animals in their winter dens.

MANAGEMENT OF THE GRIZZLY ONCE ESTABLISHED.   Should a successful
introduction of the grizzly in the Gila Wilderness be achieved, consideration will have to be given to the management of the species within
the Gila Wilderness and Forest. A first determinant is whether the
species is to be given particular or peripheral management consideration. In the latter circumstance, principle [sic] management of the
species would be directed to population management through game
regulations or population control as necessary and little overt actions
would be taken to benefit the species. Conversely, if the species were
to be given particular management consideration, management
would concern aspects both of the population and habitat considerations.

As discussed earlier, the current state of the vegetative types within
the Gila Wilderness appears quite changed from the likely character of
the Wilderness at the time of the demise of the grizzly from the area.
The principle [sic] change has been a major loss of grassland and earlier
successional stages and the loss of a fire-maintained grass ground
cover below the climax ponderosa forests. These types appear attractive to grizzly bears, and their current reduced state would suggest

that the Gila Wilderness is presently poorer grizzly range than it was during former times. If this is so, and if the grizzly is to be given major management consideration in the Wilderness, it follows that consideration should be given to breaking up and opening up the heavy forest stands of the Wilderness. In view of the current classification of the Gila Wilderness, the principle [sic] vehicle for opening the forest could be natural fire, perhaps coupled with non-control of forest insect infestations within the Wilderness. While this management option would normally be difficult to achieve inasmuch as the forest manager would be dependent upon the vagaries of natural fire occurrences, this would appear to be of limited concern in the Gila Wilderness due to the high and widespread occurrence of fire strikes.

There are, of course, a number of arguments in opposition to the non-control of insect infestations and fires in wilderness areas; however, the options of forest management in wilderness areas pretty much limit habitat manipulation to naturally occurring circumstances. Further, unless these few options are exercised, it seems probable that the resulting character of the Wilderness will be quite different than was formerly the natural state. This changed character of the Gila Wilderness would very likely not only decrease the attractiveness of the area as grizzly habitat, but for many other forms of wildlife as well.

While habitat management within the Wilderness is a logical step for improving the attractiveness and raising the support capabilities of the area for the grizzly, it follows that negative habitat management might be employed at the periphery and adjacent to the Gila Wilderness to discourage the use of these areas by the species. Ideally, the Gila Wilderness would be surrounded by an area highly unattractive to the grizzly. Where possible, such a zone could be realized by encouraging dense timber stands (Erickson, 1974), but this prospect appears limited as regards the Gila Forest. It is possible, however, that harassment conditioning, namely control or directed sport hunting at the periphery of the range, might achieve the same goal.

[1]The grizzly is but one sub-form of the European-Asian and American brown bear (*Ursus arctos*).

Bailey, V., 1931. Mammals of New Mexico. *North American Fauna*, no. 53, pp. 350–68.

Berns, V. D., and R. J. Hensel, 1972. Radio tracking brown bears on Kodiak Island. *Bears—Their Biology and Management. ICUN, Publications*, new series, no. 23, pp. 19–25.

Cowan, I. M., 1972. The status and conservation of bears (Ursidae) of the world—1970. *ICUN, Publications*, new series, no. 23, pp. 343–67.

Craighead, F. C., and J. J. Craighead, 1972. Data on grizzly bear denning activities and behavior obtained by using wildlife telemetry. *ICUN, Publications*, new series, no. 23, pp. 84–106.

———, 1964. Radio-tracking of grizzly bears in Yellowstone National Park, Wyoming, 1964. *Nat. Geo. Soc. Res. Reports, 1964 Projects*, pp. 35–43.

Curry-Lindahl, K., 1972. The brown bear (*Ursus arctos* L.) in Europe: decline, present distribution, biology and ecology. *ICUN Publications*, new series, no. 23, pp. 74–80.

Elkmork, K., 1962. Bjornen i Vassfartraktene, 1954–58. *Saertrykk av Naturen* 1, pp. 36–54.

Erickson, A. W., 1965. The brown-grizzly bear in Alaska, its ecology and management, Alaska Dept. Fish and Game. *Federal Aid in Wildlife Research*, Project Report 5, pp. 1–42.

———, 1974. Grizzly bear management in the Seeley Lake District, Lo Lo National Forest. *Contract Report, Region I, U.S. Forest Service*, pp. 22.

Hayward, B. J., 1974. Field check lists of plants and animals occurring in the Gila National Forest.

Lentfer, J. W., R. J. Hensel, L. H. Miller, L. P. Glenn and V. D. Berns, 1972. Remarks on denning habits of brown bears. *ICUN, Publications*, new series, no. 23, pp. 125–37.

Leopold, A. S., 1967. Grizzlies of the Sierra del Nido. *Pacific Discovery*, vol. 20, pp. 30–32.

———, 1958. Situacion del oso Plateado in Chihuahua. *Revista de la Sociedad Mexicana de Historia Natural*, vol. 19, pp. 115–20.

Ligon, J.S., 1917. See page 368, of Bailey, 1931.

———, 1927. Wildlife of New Mexico: its conservation and management, being a report on the game survey of the state 1926 and 1927. 212 p. *Illus. New Mex. Fish and Game Comm.*, Santa Fe.

Pearson, A. M., 1972. Population characteristics of the Northern Interior grizzly in the Yukon Territory, Canada. *ICUN Publications*, new series, no. 23, pp. 32–35.

INDEX

Walnut, 17, 25, 53, 121, 153
Warblers, 22
Warbler, Gray Black-Throated, 86
Water Canyon, 127
Weather in the Gila Country (section on), 50–54
West, Fort, 39
West Fork of Gila Trail, 113–118 (description of trail)
West Fork of Mogollon Creek, 163, 164
Whip-tailed lizard, xiii
White Creek, 44, 64, 75, 114, 115, 146, 147, 148, 169
White Rock Canyon, 152
Whitewater Baldy, 7, 79, 80
Whitewater Trail, 81–86 (description of trail)
Willow, 17, 25, 121
Willow Creek, 118
Wild Grape, 17, 53, 121
Wild Onion, 17

Wild Potato, 17
Wild Raspberry, 17, 53
Wilderness Ethic (section on), 65–67
Wood Rat, 61
Woodland Park-Meadows Trail, 146–151 (description of trail)
Woodrow, Henry (First Wilderness Ranger), 43, 44, 75, 147
Woodrow Canyon, 162
Woods, Tom, 199
Woody's Corral, 130, 152, 185
Wolf, Mexican, 47
Wolf, Gray, 18, 44, 45, 155, 156, 180
Woodpecker, Downy, 22
Wren, Canyon, 86

Yucca, 17, 22

Zig-Zag Trail, 143, 146, 180, 199